THE PERSON IN THE PULPIT

Abingdon Preacher's Library

THE PERSON IN THE PULPIT

Preaching as Caring

Willard Francis Jabusch

Abingdon Preacher's Library

William D. Thompson, Editor

ABINGDON
Nashville

THE PERSON IN THE PULPIT: PREACHING AS CARING

Copyright © 1980 by Abingdon

Second Printing 1981

Library of Congress Cataloging in Publication Data

JABUSCH, WILLARD
   The person in the pulpit.
   (Abingdon preacher's library series)
   Includes index.
   1. Preaching. I. Title
   BV4211.2.J28   251   79-28812

ISBN 0-687-30784-8

Scripture quotations unless otherwise noted are from the Revised Standard Version of the Bible, copyright 1946, 1952, © 1971, 1973 by the Division of Christian Education of the National Council of the Churches of Christ in the U.S.A.; those noted TEV are from the Bible in Today's English Version, copyright © American Bible Society 1966, 1971, 1976; those noted NEB are from the English Bible, © the Delegates of the Oxford University Press and the Syndics of the Cambridge University Press 1961, 1970.

MANUFACTURED BY THE PARTHENON PRESS AT
NASHVILLE, TENNESSEE, UNITED STATES OF AMERICA

**For my father and mother—
their lives have spoken to me of Jesus.**

CONTENTS

EDITOR'S FOREWORD

Preaching has captured the attention of increasingly large segments of the American public. Lay parish committees seeking pastoral leadership consistently rank preaching as the most desirable pastoral skill. Seminary courses and clergy conferences on preaching attract participants in larger numbers than ever. Millions of viewers watch television preachers every week.

What is *good* preaching? is the question of both those who hear it and those who do it. Hearers answer that question instinctively, tuning in the preacher who meets their needs, whether in the pulpit of the neighborhood church or on a broadcast. Preachers need to answer more intentionally.

Time was that a good, thick book on preaching would do it, or a miscellaneous smattering of thin ones. The time now seems ripe for a different kind of resource—a carefully conceived, tightly edited series of books whose scope covers the homiletical spectrum and whose individual volumes reveal the latest and best thinking about each specialty within the field of preaching. The volumes in the Abingdon Preacher's Library enable the preacher to understand preaching in its historical setting, to examine its biblical and theological underpinnings; to explore its spiritual, relational, and liturgical dimensions; and to develop insights into its craftsmanship.

Designed primarily for use in the seminary classroom, this series also will serve the practicing preacher whose background in homiletics is spotty or out-of-date, or whose preaching needs strengthening in some specific area.

> William D. Thompson
> Eastern Baptist Theological Seminary
> Philadelphia, Pennsylvania

PREFACE

Sometimes we preachers get discouraged, not so much because of worries concerning content or technique—as important as these are—and not so much because of a congregation that seems unreceptive, but rather because of who we are.

For preaching has a way of revealing our personal weaknesses. We tend to get weary, drained of physical and mental energy; we feel the weight of a weekly obligation. We start to feel guilty about our superficiality, our glib and banal words, our lack of prayer and preparation.

But most of all, in our most honest moments, we know we are really not worthy of such a role in the Christian community. The people in the pews often seem closer to the gospel than the people in the pulpits. We almost envy the janitor and the ushers whose jobs seem so simple or the organist who contributes a wordless skill. But our offering is made of words, our imperfect and fragile words. And even if our last effort seemed to have some merit, we are not at all sure we can do it again this Sunday!

We know that we ourselves are sinners in need of the hope and repentance we talk about to our brothers and sisters. We feel judged by the very words we speak. Our unhealed wounds hurt us even if we can hide them from the people. The real danger is not being puffed up with vanity but instead becoming depressed with our faults, our foolishness and our failures (and our alliteration!).

I must admit that writing this little book about the characteristics of the preacher reminded me personally that we did not start preaching because we're good, but because Jesus cared enough to call us. And we will continue doing preaching with wonder and delight only if we care about him and his people.

I. OUR BIBLICAL JOB DESCRIPTION

It takes a certain amount of "chutzpa" to stand up in a pulpit and preach! What kind of man or woman dares to give a sermon to the folks out there in the pews? An egotist? A charlatan? There have been more than a few in the history of Christianity. Jonestown was not the first place where poor people were led to destruction by a talented but evil preacher.

Is the preacher a functionary, a bureaucratic spokesperson, saying the words and taking the stipend? Jesus knew that there would be hirelings, indifferent, insouciant, "quid pro quo" preachers, heartless and bored.

Or, is the preacher a prophet, a reformer, a visionary, a revolutionary whose words sizzle like acid in the minds of the complacent? A lean and hungry preacher with fire burning in the entrails? From Jeremiah through Savonarola to Dom Helder Camara in the arid northeast of Brazil, the line of preachers who tear away the mask of hypocrisy is a long and noble one.

Or is the preacher a saint? A holy person who walks with the Lord, listens to his voice, and tells of what has been heard and seen? Thomas Aquinas felt that the preacher's task was *contemplare et aliis tradere contemplata*: to contemplate and to bring to others what has been contemplated. Is the preacher a "guru," or spiritual leader? One who is pure of heart and virtuous of life? There have been preachers who are examples of heroic sanctity.

These are only a few of the kinds of people who have attempted to preach to the people. There are many models, some clearly bad, others highly suspicious, still others most attractive and laudable, and some almost impossibly exalted! What is today's seminary student to think about the variety of persons who have inhabited the Christian pulpit; how may the young preacher shun what is evil and imitate what is good from the experience of the past?

In this little book we will not examine what the preacher has to say or how it is said. We will not investigate the nature of the sermon, the theology of preaching, or theories of communication. We will not attempt an analysis of the audience. Instead, we will look at the person of the preacher, who it is who stands in the pulpit of a Christian church and dares to speak. It is, I think, a most important undertaking.

There is an old maxim in philosophy: *agere sequitur esse*, which might be translated as, one's actions follow from one's being. What you do (and what you say) follow from what you are. Good preaching comes from good people. If the Christian church would hope to be blessed with good preaching on Sundays, it must be deeply concerned with the character of its preachers, and the quality of their lives on the other days of the week.

A young couple told me recently about their experiences on the committee to interview and choose a new pastor. They were not impressed with the quality of the candidates; some seemed selfish and demanding, others were more than a little bizarre, and at least one confessed that he had no faith at all! He admitted that he was a preacher because he really couldn't get another job—an agnostic willing to proclaim the gospel to keep food on the table!

"Did you finally select someone?" I asked.

"Yes," they said. "He really is a klutz however. He dropped the altar breads all over the floor, and one Sunday he actually fell off the chair in the chancel! But we love him. He visits the sick. The children adore him. He's kind and unpretentious and very generous with his time. He's not a very good preacher, in fact, he's quite bad, but we can put up with that."

What they would not put up with, of course, was a hireling, selfish, cold, unbelieving. They were ready and willing to tolerate a

klutz in their pulpit rather than a clever trickster or a slick and
ambitious playboy. They were very much concerned about the ethos
of their preacher.

THE ETHOS OF THE PREACHER

The concept of ethos is very old indeed. Aristotle wrote in *The Rhetoric:*

> Of proofs provided by the speech there are three kinds: one kind
> depending on the character of the speaker; another, on disposing the
> hearer in a certain way; a third, a demonstration or apparent
> demonstration in the speech itself. Ethical proof is wrought when the
> speech is so spoken as to make the speaker credible; for we trust good
> men more and sooner, as a rule, about everything; while, about
> things which do not admit of precision, but only of guess-work, we
> trust them absolutely. . . . It is not true, as some of the technical
> writers assume in their systems, that the moral worth of the speaker
> contributes nothing to his persuasiveness; nay, it might be said that
> almost the most authoritative of proofs is that supplied by character.[1]

For the ancient Greeks, *logos,* the reasoning, the logic of an
argument, was not to be despised; *pathos,* the appeal to the emotions
of the audience, was certainly important. But it would seem that
ethos, the character or reputation of the speaker, was the most
important element of all.

Quintilian, in the *Institutio Oratoria,* has no doubts about the
worth of the individual communicator and the ethical standards
which he needs to adopt:

> The orator then, whom I am concerned to form, shall be the orator as
> defined by Marcus Cato, "a good man, skilled in speaking." But
> above all he must possess the quality which Cato places first and
> which is in the very nature of things the greatest and most important,
> that is, he must be a good man. This is essential not merely on
> account of the fact that, if the powers of eloquence serve only to lend
> arms to crime, there can be nothing more pernicious than eloquence
> to public and private welfare alike.[2]

The early Christian preachers, themselves so often formed by the
great Greek and Latin rhetorical traditions, were even more inclined

to stress the preacher's life and wisdom as more important than mere eloquence. (Today's female preachers—and their number is happily growing—will have to be tolerant of many early writers and speakers. Although the first preachers of the resurrection were the women who hurried back from the empty tomb to proclaim the good news, men have dominated the preaching ministry for many centuries; almost all references, therefore, tend to suppose that the preacher is masculine.) St. Augustine expands on the wisdom necessary for preaching:

> For a man speaks more or less wisely to the extent that he has become more or less proficient in the Holy Scriptures. I do not speak of the man who has read widely and memorized much, but of the man who has well understood and has diligently sought out the sense of the Scriptures. For there are those who read them and neglect them, who read that they may remember but neglect them in that they fail to understand them. Those are undoubtedly to be preferred who remember the words less well, but who look into the heart of the Scriptures with the eye of their own hearts. But better than either of these is he who can quote them when he wishes and understands them properly.[3]

St. Augustine, well trained in classical rhetoric, had no argument with Cato's pithy definition of an orator, "a good man, skilled in speaking," but he said the Christian speaker must go further; he or she must look profoundly at sacred Scripture, "look into the heart of the Scriptures with the eye of their own hearts." If we would understand the character of the Christian preacher—what kind of a person he or she is meant to be—we also must begin with the New Testament.

I am reluctant to believe that English is a less rich and flexible language than Greek, but the fact remains that New Testament Greek uses a variety of words to express what we mean by the one word "preacher." It is clearly important for us to look at the terms used to describe preachers and what they do in the New Testament.

Frequently, their preaching is simply called "speaking." It is a humble term, found particularly in Luke's writings, but this speaking has a new and wonderful content. Jesus, for example, "spoke to them of the kingdom of God" (Luke 9:11). Paul would speak of "the mystery of Christ" (Col. 4:3). There is a prophetic character to much of what is spoken: the word of the Lord, the word of the good news, the word of salvation and the cross, the word of grace and the Kingdom. These preachers were speakers in the name of God.

In John's Gospel, "speaking" is the usual expression (together with "teaching") for the preaching of Jesus, and it is tied in with the theme of the sending of Jesus by the Father. But, of the thirty-two verbs used by the New Testament authors to express preaching, there are others which indicate the preacher's task more vividly.

THE PREACHER AS HERALD

An important synonym we use when translating the Greek verb for preaching is "to proclaim" or "to herald." Those who were healed by Jesus "proclaimed" what the Lord had done for them (Mark 1:4; 5:20; 7:36).

A new and wonderful happening is announced. God's kingdom is proclaimed; the poor have the good news preached to them. John appeared in the wilderness and proclaimed a baptism of repentance for the forgiveness of sins (Mark 1:4), and then Jesus himself came into Galilee and proclaimed the gospel of God (Mark 1:14), and the gospel of the kingdom (Matt. 4:23). He told his followers to declare that the kingdom of heaven is at hand (Matt. 10:7), and to go into the world proclaiming the gospel to the whole creation (Mark 16:15).

It is to be a public announcement; what Jesus told them is to be proclaimed upon the housetops (Matt. 10:27). Certainly Paul saw himself as a herald who proclaimed the gospel of God (1 Thess. 2:9; 1 Tim. 1:11, cf. also 1 Tim. 2:7). The preaching of the apostles was "a proclamation of the death, resurrection and exaltation of Jesus, that led to an evaluation of His person as both Lord and Christ, confronted man with the necessity of repentance, and promised the forgiveness of sins."[4]

But what did it mean to be a herald who went about proclaiming? What was the role of the secular herald? He was the mouthpiece of his master who, like a town crier in the marketplace, proclaimed what he was told to say. He spoke in the name of his master and with his power and authority.

However, it was also very clear to every herald that he was in no way to modify, subtract, or add anything to the message. He was sent on diplomatic missons from one Greek city-state to another and was supposed to be protected by the gods and immune from attack. However, he was not a negotiator or a legate with freedom to discuss or compromise. He could, in fact, be punished if he did not transmit his master's message exactly as it was given. He had no personal significance; he was valued only for his message.

It is this title of "herald" that has been much featured in contemporary writing. There has been great interest in kerygmatic theology and preaching. In fact, preaching is sometimes exclusively identified with proclamation and the single title of "herald" is used to define the preacher. It seems to me that this is unfortunate. For all of the meaning and power which this title does contain, it is not the only one which can give the preacher a sense of identity. It is good to remember that it is used as a title only in the Pauline writings, and then only twice. Was this because of the immunity from contradiction which is included in the Greek meaning of the term? Jesus had clearly told his disciples that they could expect to be persecuted vigorously (Matt. 10:16). Whereas the herald was always to be listened to respectfully and to be honored, the hard realities of apostolic preaching brought tribulations and suffering (Acts 4:5-21; 5:21-41; 2 Cor. 11:23-33).

Undue emphasis on this title can also lead to an artificial and static quality in preaching. If the preacher as herald is only to repeat the words of the master and exclude all personal elements, then creative preaching is really not necessary. All that would be required is a corps of lectors with loud and persistent voices who could repeat over and over the very words of the Bible.

The title rightly stresses the fact that the preacher is entrusted with a message from God. But it also excludes any personal style of presentation. The herald has no freedom to adapt to various audiences; he must merely repeat by rote what he has been told to say. Personality must be suppressed and nothing must be changed, even the very words of the communication. The herald becomes a sort of mechanical recording, shouting out a memorized message, unconcerned about the feelings and attitudes of the hearers or the special situations in which the message must be announced. The preaching of a classical herald quickly could become inhuman, forced, and sterile. And, although proclamation certainly means something powerful and urgent in both Greek and English, it is only a short step from proclamation to declamation, with all the pomposity and artificiality that is implied in that word.

I remember hearing of a survey that was made among a group of parishioners. They were asked to write down what they hoped to experience during a sermon. If the pollsters expected some profound Christian hope, they were probably disappointed! For the majority of the people had a very modest expectation. They wanted to experience "a man speaking." Just that. It sounds rather obvious and unexciting, certainly a bare minimum. (Today, especially if their consciousness had been raised regarding woman's liberation and sexist language, they might have asked for a "person speaking.") They wanted to experience a live human being who feels pain and happiness, who has good days and bad days, who is something less than perfect, and who is *speaking*. Not declaiming a text which is not his own; not proclaiming a message, even a holy message, in an especially loud and unusual voice; not spitting out Bible texts like a noisy mechanical doll; not shouting or orating or chanting or moaning. Just speaking. Perhaps it seemed to this group of parishioners almost too much to hope for! They had experienced, perhaps, too many puppets, too many cardboard preachers, indifferent, cold, heartless, and ultimately cruel. Words had been thrown at them like stones. The very phrases of the Gospel had been drained of their color and zest and ladled out like a tasteless gray broth. All they were looking for at this point was a real human being who could gently and modestly speak.

The herald certainly represents one aspect of the preacher's being, but, just as the New Testament authors, we must be cautious and never let this particular title lead us into contempt for the variety of audiences and the need to adapt the divine message. The Christian herald must always be perceived as "a person speaking."

THE PREACHER AS SERVANT

St. Paul uses another title in reference to preaching the gospel. Paul says he has become a "servant of the church" since he must

preach the word of God (Col. 1:25 TEV). And Timothy is told that if
he preaches as Paul tells him, he will be a good "servant of Christ" (1
Tim. 4:6 TEV). Paul says that he is himself a "servant of the gospel"
(Eph. 3:7; Col. 1:23 TEV) and that he and his helpers are "servants
of the new covenant" (2 Cor. 3:6 TEV).

While the word *diakonos* is used in the gospels to underline the need
for humility, Paul uses the word to stress not only humility but also
urgent service in the cause of the Christian mission, the noble task
which he has been given (2 Tim. 4:2; 2 Cor. 5:14). He calls Timothy
"our brother and God's servant in the gospel of Christ" (1 Thess. 3:2).
The whole apostolate is referred to as a ministry, or service, "the
ministry of the word" (Acts 6:4). It is a priestly service of the gospel: "the
grace given me by God to be a minister of Christ Jesus to the Gentiles in
the priestly service of the gospel of God, so that the offering of the
Gentiles may be acceptable, sanctified by the Holy Spirit" (Rom.
15:15-16). But, although the service of the gospel is holy and priestly, it
is always a service, the work of humble servants, of those who minister
and not of those who rule. We are "servants through whom you
believed, as the Lord assigned to each" (1 Cor. 3:5). The *diakonos* is no
better than the waiters who served the meal and poured the wine at the
marriage feast at Cana. The *diakonos* does his master's bidding and
must see that the guests are served.

Even more striking, perhaps, is Paul's use of the term "slave" to
describe the preacher. He applies it to himself (Rom. 1:1 *mar. a*) and to
his collaborators (Phil. 1:1 *mar. a*; Col. 4:12 *mar. g*; 2 Tim. 2:24). It is
a term of great humility and abasement, but it is also necessary to note
that the "slave of Christ" is the *'ebed Yahweh* of the New Testament and
means that God has chosen Paul as his own instrument, or agent, in
the working out of his divine plan of salvation (1 Cor. 3:5 NEB). In the
Old Testament, *'ebed Yahweh* was a term of highest honor, not
because of any personal merit of the "slave of God," but because
Yahweh had designated a lowly human being as his instrument. God
had no need of Cyrus: "Apart from me, all is nothing" (Isa. 45:6); but,
in his goodness and wisdom he decided to make use of Israel: "Hear,
O—Jacob my slave, Israel whom I have chosen" (Isa. 44: 1).

The pomp and pretentions of the clergy seem especially foolish
when we begin to understand that preachers are meant to be servants

and slaves! The self-important preacher, puffed up by the flattery of overly generous parishioners, is all too well known. Some are perceived by lay people as lords (or ladies!) of the manor, because, in fact, the preachers no longer see themselves as lowly servants. It is not difficult for seminarians or junior clergy to point to older pastors who seem to have forgotten the root meaning of ministry, yet the seeds of arrogance and vanity may already have begun to sprout in their own lives. The title of minister is given today to men and women, both young and old, who would reject the synonymous title of servant or slave. To be a minister, at least until recently, is to be honored, respected, reverenced by society; the word sounds serenely on the tongue and has an almost unctuous quality. But to be a slave? Are we willing to spend long and laborious days in the service of the word of God when the rest of our generation follows a "me-first" philosophy of taking care of "number one." Ours is the age of self-satisfaction, not of self-denial; of complete fulfillment, not of abnegation. Christ may have emptied himself, taking the form of a slave, but his followers are not inclined to do the same. The slave, or servant, image of the preacher is probably the most distasteful one for the contemporary imagination.

THE PREACHER AS STEWARD

If preaching involves the humble and totally obedient service of a slave of Christ, there is another title, that of "steward," or "manager," which allows for much more initiative. *Oikonomos* denotes the slave charged with the distribution of rations (Luke 12:42). The *Greek–English Lexicon of the New Testament* by Grimm and Thayer gives this definition: "The manager of a household or of household affairs; especially a steward, manager, superintendent . . . to whom the head of a house or proprietor has entrusted the management of his affairs, the care of receipts and expenditures, and the duty of dealing out the proper portion to every servant and even to the children not yet of age."[5]

Paul speaks of himself and Apollos as "stewards of the mysteries of God" (1 Cor. 4:1). And, as stewards, it is their job and that of the preachers who follow to see that the household is served the food that will nourish and strengthen everyone. A steward brings out the proper kind of food and the proper amount of food according to the season and the needs of all the children and the servants; the steward has received an important trust, and he must show himself worthy of it.

Moreover, the larder from which the Christian preacher and steward brings out what is needed is filled with very special things indeed—the "mysteries of God." John Stott remarks: "*Mysterion* in the New Testament is not a dark, unexplained enigma, but a truth which has been made known, which can only be known because God has disclosed it, which has been hitherto concealed but is now revealed, and into which God has initiated men. So 'the mysteries of God' are God's open secrets, the sum total of His self-revelation which is now embodied in the Scriptures."[6]

We have been entrusted with these great and beautiful mysteries which can bring such hope and happiness when we bring them out at the proper time and share them with the people for whom we are responsible. Though, as stewards of the household, we must distribute the "food," we do not have to supply it! We are not forced to come up with some novel message, some new wisdom which is the product of our own brain. The Lord has stocked the Christian larder, as it were, and we must bring out the nourishment that is needed for the here and now.

Clearly, there is to be no waste or foolishness in dispensing the goods which have been left in our charge. We are to guard what is so precious; there must be no watering down of the mysteries, no tampering with the message. If the household is in need of strong meat, it is not for us to try to make it soft and insipid. Paul said, "I did not shrink from declaring to you the whole counsel of God" (Acts 20:27). "The household of God urgently needs faithful stewards who will dispense to it systematically the whole Word of God, not the New Testament only, but the Old as well, not the best known texts only, but also the less known, not just the passages which favour the preacher's particular prejudices, but those which do not!"[7]

Many things follow if one is to be a truly worthy steward. There will be careful planning, an imaginative "serving up" of what the people need so that their appetite will be stimulated and their jaded palates rejoice in a taste that is fresh and delightful. It may be necessary to persuade the children of the household to eat what is good for them, but even this can be done with the greatest possible creativity and charm. The diet for all should be well-balanced, palatable, full of zest and interest. For some a very special menu may be indicated. A good steward is aware of the problems and needs, the weaknesses and predilections of those whom he serves. "Who then is the faithful and wise steward, whom his master will set over his household, to give them their portion of food at the proper time?"(Luke 12:42).

One Sunday night some years ago, I was walking past All Souls Church on Langham Place in central London. It was a summer evening and the sound of vigorous hymn singing and the light from the windows drew me to the front door. I was greeted by a friendly usher who told me that all the seats on the first floor were occupied, but if I would go up the stairs to the gallery another usher would find me a seat. I was given a hymn book and guided to what was probably the last available seat in the gallery. The sermon, one in a Sunday night series on the parables of Jesus, was just beginning; the preacher was an Anglican pastor, the Reverend John R. W. Stott, and his text was the parable of the prodigal son. As I looked down into the crowded nave and around the packed gallery of the church, I saw a household that was hungry for the food of the gospel. The predominantly young congregation was mostly British, of course, but there were also a goodly number of Asiatics, Africans, and West Indians. Most were, I suspect, young singles who were living in London, unsure of themselves and their future, frustrated and fearful, dismayed by the sophistication and the crudeness, the competition and the loneliness of life in one of the world's largest cities. How many of them were themselves prodigal sons and daughters, who had left home for a distant city of allure and disillusion?

John Stott proved himself to be a wise and prudent steward of the mysteries of God. His words were warm and compassionate, for he truly loved the members of the household. And his words revealed the challenge and beauty and hope of the gospel parable, for he clearly knew the kind of nourishment which this London congregation needed. His style was simple and direct without frills or strained effects; after all, this was a hungry congregation in search of real food.

After the sermon and the final hymn and prayer, some young people nearby warmly invited me, a Yankee stranger, to a Bible study group meeting on Tuesday evening. Here was a congregation that was lively, engaged, reaching out with enthusiasm and joy to share something good which had been discovered. Here were men and women being nourished by the mysteries of God and obviously finding the experience satisfying and vitally important. One hears a lot about the empty churches of England, but it would certainly seem that the household turns out in great numbers when there is a good steward in the pulpit!

THE PREACHER AS FATHER

Any title can become common, empty of meaning, and tossed about without a thought of its original impact. Like a coin that has been rubbed smooth, its inscription can no longer be seen, and it slips almost too easily between the fingers. As a Catholic priest, I can say with certainty that the title "Father" is often used by both laity and priests in the most casual of ways. When, somewhere back in the distant past, people in certain countries began to call their priests "Mon Père" or "Padre" or "Father", it surely had a special resonance which it lacks today. And yet the title is beautiful and an apt one for a male preacher if he can say with Paul: "You know how, like a father with his children, we exhorted each one of you and encouraged you and charged you to lead a life worthy of God" (1 Thess. 2:11-12). For as John Stott points out, "St Paul did not hesitate to call himself the 'father' of the Corinthians, the Galatians and the Thessalonians, as well as of certain individuals, and there is no doubt that a father's qualities, particularly of gentleness and love, which the Apostle mentions, are indispensable to the preacher as portrayed in the New Testament."[8]

Even a good steward may serve the household only out of duty; a good father serves his family out of love and with deep affection. A father belongs to his children in a way that no steward belongs to the members of the household. Stewards may be interchangeable;

fathers are not, as so many have sadly discovered. Is it, in fact, possible to define the limits of a good father's love?

Some time ago communications theory specialists discovered that, although fear is a potent motivation to exploit in advertising, there is a definite threshold beyond which it is not profitable to go. For example, at a certain point the lurid descriptions of what will happen to your lungs if you continue to smoke no longer register; you have passed the threshold of fear, and it is impossible to scare you further on this subject. Thousands of people have read frightening stories and seen horror pictures, but they still light up another cigarette! Research has also turned up a most interesting exception, however.

Although, when the threshold of fear is passed, a person will not be moved to do something for his own safety, if it is a question of the well-being of his children, there simply is no threshold of fear! Fear as a motivation can be pushed all the way, as many fire detector and life insurance commercials vividly demonstrate. It seems that a father really does worry about his children and will do and buy almost anything to protect them.

If we accept Paul's simile of "father," it follows that the preacher is to have this less than reasonable kind of love for his congregation. It is a love that goes to extremes, at least on certain occasions, love that prompts the preacher to go to any lengths to protect his "children," a love that is not easily measured and which does not count the cost.

Is the use of this title, and all that it could mean for the attitude of the preacher, too daring and too dangerous? After all, Jesus said: "Call no man your father on earth, for you have one Father, who is in heaven" (Matt. 23:9). Clearly, we are not to compete with the heavenly Father; we are to have no sense of superiority nor dare to usurp divine glory and authority for ourselves.

Stott rightly says, "I suggest that what Jesus is saying is that we are never to adopt towards a fellow man in the Church the attitude of dependence which a child has towards his father, nor are we to require others to be or become spiritually dependent on us."[9] We are not to be paternalistic preachers, keeping the people childish. The temptation to keep clients dependent and immature is quite frankly a very real one in the helping professions. When, as I write this, the going rate for psychologists is $45 for an hour of consultation and $95 for an hour with a psychiatrist, it is easy to see why some prolong the sessions and encourage dependency. Although the pastor-preacher may not ask a fee for his advice and helping words, he may for unworthy reasons want to be a father who refuses to let his children grow up. His will and the will of God have been identified in his mind; he has become a sacred despot. To question him is to question God. He knows that only cowed and pliable children will give him the blind obedience which he demands. It is necessary to keep them docile and weak.

But all of this is a far cry from Paul and what the "father-child" metaphor meant to him:

> I do not write this to make you ashamed, but to admonish you as my beloved children. For though you have countless guides in Christ, you do not have many fathers. For I became your father in Christ Jesus through the gospel. I urge you, then, be imitators of me. Therefore I sent to you Timothy, my beloved and faithful child in the Lord, to remind you of my ways in Christ, as I teach them everywhere in every church. (1 Cor. 4:14-17)

If Paul became the Corinthians' "father in Christ Jesus through the gospel," the preacher of that same gospel today becomes a father too. (Or, in the case of a female preacher, a "mother." St. Paul uses only the male metaphor, but then goes on to ask, "Shall I come to you with a rod, or with love in the spirit of gentleness" (v. 21)? The emphasis here is on qualities which are common to both parents.)

The parent-child relationship is intimate, warmly affectionate, but not incompatible with the difficult words and actions which are sometimes necessary. The father and mother will have great happiness as they watch the growth and accomplishments of the child; they are proud parents who speak glowingly and freely of what their child has achieved and are quick to show the pictures which they carry in their wallets. But they also know pain and worry. If the happiness of a parent is something very special as he or she rejoices over the goodness and charm of the child, it is equally true that the sorrow that a parent may sometimes feel is like a sword piercing the heart.

Any exploration of the joys and sorrows of parenthood and the qualities of a good father and mother can teach us something of the relationship between the preacher and his or her "beloved children." The love of a parent which has a difficult time admitting any limits, which is tender, enduring, so gentle and understanding, and which is probably the most powerful of New Testament metaphors for the preacher, can be a model for everyone who has the responsibility of preaching the gospel.

Even before John Chrysostom became bishop of Constantinople, he proved that he was a true father of his people. He had been ordained presbyter or helper of the bishop of Antioch in 386, and a year later a rebellion broke out in the city protesting extreme taxation. The statues of the imperial family were toppled and dragged through the streets by the rioting crowd. The Emperor Theodosius was not amused! Once order was restored, all knew that the royal wrath would be fierce and without mercy; the folly of one day of statue-smashing by some irate young citizens could lead to a frightening punishment for the whole city. John Chrysostom, unlike so many others, did not flee. He stayed with those who could not, for various reasons, run away, and each day he would preach to them as they awaited the imperial fury. He was a father among his fearful children, and he spoke words of real comfort. He shared their affliction, but his words helped to give a Christian meaning to their terror; and, like a good father, he called them to be courageous and to behave in a worthy way. The city was stricken, it was true, but it was also a time to begin a new life, to repent, and to have hope! He preached as a strong and gentle father would to some very unruly children, not excusing their misdemeanors, but also not abandoning them to despair.

Recently a girl of nineteen, who had spoken of suicide, left her home in Libertyville, Illinois. She took a bottle of sleeping pills with her and was seen walking into a heavily wooded area. All night and all the next day, her father accompanied the police as they searched the area, carefully looking for her in every possible place. The preacher who is a father (or mother) for the people does not remain aloof, unconcerned, waiting for the church to be filled so that a sermon can be delivered; rather he or she goes into the woods, looking for those who are lost and confused.

Vincent de Paul, for example, could have had a comfortable life preaching urbane sermons to the aristocratic household of Philippe Emmanuel de Gondi, Comte de Joigny and general of the royal galleys of France. He would have been no different from many other harmless house chaplains to the noble families, acting as tutor for their spoiled children and spiritual guide for their bored and self-indulgent souls. However, when he accompanied his employer on a voyage on one of the royal galleys and saw the galley-slaves chained and flogged at their benches, he knew that his life and his preaching could never be the same. It was 1619, a time of plague and war, of a peasantry living in misery and a few great lords and ladies living in crass luxury. Vincent began—at the age of fifty!—to seek out the poorest of the poor and to preach with a new simplicity the necessity of Christian service. In this age of elaborate pulpit oratory and Baroque extravagance, the sermons of Vincent de Paul come as a surprise and a shock. They do not read well; they are not models of rhetoric; there is no attempt at a beautiful style. They seem today in their printed form somewhat banal, and we find ourselves wondering why they had such a powerful effect. And they did have a great effect. For the first time in France, people began to look after little children, the hundreds of unwanted children left on the doorstep or under the bridges of the city. For the first time in Paris, men and women devoted their lives to the care of the mentally defective. Fashionable women left the sham and insincerity of their lives at court to tend to the sick in the hospitals which Vincent established for the physically ill, for the criminals from the galleys with infectious diseases, and for the insane. He told them they must know no convent but the sickroom, no cloister but the street. Vincent demanded much because he gave much. His life and his preaching were one. He was known by both the royal family and thousands of miserable paupers as *le bon M. Vincent,* not only because he was good, but because he was good in a most loveable and vivacious way. Although he got a rather late start, he quickly became a father who sought out his children, kind but with no trace of condescension in his kindness, uncompromising in his demands on those who would follow him in service of the poor, audacious as he went to the galley-slaves, the prisoners, and the sick.

If his sermons lack elegance and fire in print, it is because we do not catch the glance of his eyes, wistful and humorous, or the tone of his voice, so shrewd and affectionate; we do not see the daily example of his life of fatherly love.

In the United States today, perhaps Vincent de Paul is best known because a large Chicago university has been named after him. But in the history of Christianity, he must be remembered as a preacher with all the qualities of a good father. He sought out his children, not waiting for them to come to him. He spoke with great simplicity in order that they could understand and respond. He challenged them, and he comforted them. And, most important of all, he taught them by his example, for, as any good father knows, that is the most potent form of instruction.

THE PREACHER AS GOD'S COWORKER

Of all the preacher's titles, that of father has the warmest connotations and says the most about the kind of love which the people have a right to expect from us. But there is another title which has much to say about the love which God has for those called to preach. Paul and Apollos (1 Cor. 3:9) and Timothy (1 Thess. 3:2) are given this beautiful and daring title which expresses so well the role of the preacher in God's saving work. *Sunergos theou* means God's coworker, the one who collaborates with God. Could there be a greater dignity? Could any work be more noble and worthy? Could any vocation be as wonderful?

In 1 Thess. 3:2, Paul says that he has sent Timothy, "our brother and God's coworker in the gospel of Christ, to establish you and encourage your faith." As Jerome Murphy-O'Connor has written: "Here the sphere of collaboration is determined by the phrase 'in the gospel of Christ.' 'Gospel' obviously must be taken in the active sense it enjoys in 1 Thess. 2:14; Phil. 1:5; and Rom. 1:1, that is, as the actual communication of the good news of salvation. It is precisely as a preacher, therefore, that Timothy is God's cooperator."[10]

Collaborators and cooperators work closely together. If two people are working together, for example, on the music and lyrics of a new Broadway musical, they must understand each other's style and approach. They must meet frequently. They must spend long hours together discussing the work in progress. They must agree on a thousand minute details long after there has been agreement and clarity on theme and plot and mood. If, let us say, Richard Rodgers asked a young and unknown songwriter to collaborate with him on a new show, writing the lyrics for Rodgers' beautiful and winning melodies, it would imply great confidence and respect for the new talent. There would also be a certain risk involved.

It would seem that in the very important project of salvation, God is willing to take a risk with some unlikely helpers. He has a trust in us and a respect for us that we do not have for ourselves or each other. He is ready to use us to convey his message to men and women, knowing—as he surely does—our weakness, our foolishness, and our awkward limitations. It is a great mystery which every preacher must face: that God would use the likes of me as his coworker!

> The preacher is a paradox. He is a man of destiny but not master of his own. He is devoid of personal significance but a key figure in the salvation of the world. He teaches with authority and freedom but is essentially a simple organ of communication. He can speak of the message he brings as 'his', but it does not originate with him nor does he have any power over it. He is chosen from among men and given a title of honour, but his privilege is to serve and to suffer. He is a slave but motivated by love."[11]

Perhaps it is this title of God's coworker which helps us to understand the paradox. "The preacher is only the spokesman of another, but because that other is God, to be chosen to collaborate with him, no matter what be the conditions of service, is to be honoured and not degraded. The preacher is only an administrator, but the deposit entrusted to him is the word of life."[12]

II. VOICES OF THE PIONEERS

At an ecumenical gathering, one minister confided to me over coffee and cake, "Most people in my denomination think that preaching started in the sixteenth century!" All of us, no matter what our church, may sometimes forget the two thousand year history of Christian preaching and all that it can teach us. We follow in the footsteps of holy and heroic ministers of the word, Paul and Barnabas in the first century, Ignatius of Antioch and Polycarp in the second, Ireneus and Cyprian in the third, Basil and Ambrose in the fourth, Patrick and Leo the Great in the fifth, John I and Benedict in the sixth, Augustine of Canterbury and Columbanus in the seventh, Bede and Boniface in the eighth, Ansgar, Cyril and Methodius in the ninth—the list could go on and on! And the amazing thing is this: as we move into the age of electronic immediacy and a renewal of oral communication and away from the formal and print-dominated culture of the nineteenth century, and as we find ourselves in this strange time of unrest and massive changes—so unlike the security and comfort of the Victorian era—we suddenly discover that we are much closer to the sensibilities of these early preachers than we are to those of a hundred years ago. The political turmoil in Milan which formed the background for the work of Ambrose may be more real for us than the world of President McKinley. We have a much greater sympathy for Ansgar, facing the pagan Scandinavians, and for Cyril and his brother, Methodius, with their creative approaches in the evangelization of the Slavic peoples, than we have for the cozy pulpit pieties of our recent past.

From out of our Christian history come voices which speak to us with an urgency and a vitality which we did not suspect. Although their examples may sometimes seem quaint and their biblical scholarship quite deficient, they address us as fellow preachers who have reflected seriously on what it means to be in the service of God's holy word. Long before us, they too have struggled with the problem of the preacher's identity. With refreshing directness they point out the possible vices and the needed virtues. They are pastoral and practical, never academic or merely theoretical. Since they are themselves all involved in the care of souls, they appreciate both the beauty and the danger of their calling. They want to be good preachers themselves, and they want to help others in this noble work. What do they say to us?

AUGUSTINE

Of all the people who lived around the year 400, we probably know Augustine the best. Thanks to recent excavations under the piazza in front of the cathedral of Milan, we can even see the baptismal pool in which he was baptized by Bishop Ambrose. But few people of any age have left an autobiography as honest and as beautiful as Augustine's *Confessions*.

As Bishop of Hippo in north Africa, he preached constantly. During those thirty-five busy years, he would at times be called to preach for five consecutive days. His sermons on the Scriptures, transcribed as they were delivered, make up his many books of commentary on the Bible. The men who were formed in his monastic community themselves often became bishops and spread the influence of their great and zealous teacher.

However, it is in book four of Augustine's *De Doctrina Christiana* that we find this genius of Christian antiquity and highly talented preacher giving this instruction:

> And so our Christian orator, while he says what is just, and holy, and good (and he ought never to say anything else), does all he can to be

heard with intelligence, with pleasure, and with obedience; and he
need not doubt that if he succeed in this object, and so far as he
succeeds he will succeed more by piety in prayer than by gifts of
oratory; and so he ought to pray for himself and for those he is about to
address, before he attempts to speak. And when the hour is come that
he must speak, he ought, before he opens his mouth, to lift up his
thirsty soul to God, to drink in what he is about to pour forth, and to
be himself filled with what he is about to distribute. For, as in regard
to every matter of faith and love there are many things that may be
said and many ways of saying them, who knows what it is expedient at
a given moment for us to say, or to be heard saying, except God Who
knows the hearts of all? And who can make us say what we ought, and
in the way we ought, except Him in Whose hand both we and our
speeches are? Accordingly, he who is anxious both to know and to
teach should learn all that is to be taught, and acquire such a faculty
of speech as is suitable for a divine. But when the hour for speech
arrives, let him reflect upon that saying of our Lord's, as better suited
to the wants of a pious mind: "Take no thought how or what ye shall
speak; for it shall be given you in that same hour what ye shall speak.
For it is not ye that speak, but the Spirit of your Father which speaketh
in you". The Holy Spirit, then, speaks thus in those who for Christ's
sake are delivered to the persecutors; why not also in those who deliver
Christ's message to those who are willing to learn?[1]

Augustine does not say that prayer is the only preparation for the
preacher, just that it is the most important preparation. The preacher
is not to consider himself above and beyond the message which he
preaches; he himself is to be filled with the gospel which he
distributes to the people. He also preaches to himself.

Although Augustine is prepared to admit that an evil preacher can
do some good through his words, he would far prefer that his life be
in harmony with those words in order that the sermon have a still
greater effect:

But whatever may be the majesty of the style, the life of the speaker
will count for more in securing the hearer's compliance. The man
who speaks wisely and eloquently, but lives wickedly, may, it is true,
instruct many who are anxious to learn; though, as it is written, he "is
unprofitable to himself." Wherefore, also the apostle says: "Whether
in pretence or in truth Christ is preached." Now Christ is the truth;
yet we see that the truth can be preached, though not in truth—that
is, what is right and true in itself may be preached by a man of perverse

and deceitful mind. And thus it is that Jesus Christ is preached by those that seek their own, and not the things that are Jesus Christ's. But since true believers obey the voice, not of any man, but of the Lord Himself, Who says, "All therefore whatsoever they bid you observe, that observe and do: but do not ye after their works; for they say and do not"; therefore it is that men who themselves lead unprofitable lives are heard with profit by others. . . . Now these men do good to many by preaching what they themselves do not perform; but they would do good to very many more if they lived as they preach. For there are numbers who seek an excuse for their own evil lives in comparing the teaching with the conduct of their instructors, and who say in their hearts, or even go a little further, and say with their lips: "Why do you not do yourself what you bid me do?" And thus they cease to listen with submission to a man who does not listen to himself, and in despising the preacher they learn to despise the word that is preached. Wherefore the apostle, writing to Timothy, after telling him, "Let no man despise thy youth," adds immediately the course by which he would avoid contempt: "but be thou an example of the believers, in word, in conversation, in charity, in spirit, in faith, in purity."[2]

Augustine, who had studied rhetoric as a youth in Tagaste and Carthage and later held the municipal chair of rhetoric at Milan, knew the power of eloquence and all the means of obtaining it. He argued that it was perfectly lawful for a Christian teacher to use the art of rhetoric and to begin early in life to acquire rhetorical skill. A teacher should aim at perspicuity, beauty, and persuasiveness in all the varied styles of speaking. Augustine would hope that the preacher would speak in a way which is both elegant and forcible. His own sermons, at least in the original Latin, reveal much of the eloquence of a Cicero with a witty mix of puns and a frequent playing with sounds and meanings. But this learned bishop and founder of a monastic tradition expected something more from himself and those who would follow his direction—a dedication to prayer and holiness of life.

GREGORY NAZIANZEN AND JOHN CHRYSOSTOM

In the Greek-speaking cities to the east of Hippo, two holy and talented men were preaching and reflecting on their ministry. The most famous was, of course, the man who would be ever known as the "golden-mouthed," John Chrysostom. Less well known was a man who had been ordained against his will, had fled into the solitude of Pontus to live as a monk, but later returned to what he came to believe was truly a divine call to an active ministry. Gregory Nazianzen explained his position in a composition, usually referred to by its Latin title, *De Fuga*. He knows fully how perilous his vocation is and the judgment in store for all of those who betray their incomparable trust as leaders of the people of God. Not only his own salvation but that of others is at stake. After all, how is a true priest to be formed?

> Who can mould, as clay-figures are modelled in a single day, the defender of the truth, who is to take his stand with angels, and give glory with archangels, and cause the sacrifice to ascend to the altar on high, and share the Priesthood of Christ, and renew the creature, and set forth the image, and create inhabitants for the world above, aye, and, greatest of all be God and make others God?[3]

No wonder that he fled from such a responsibility!

> But his attention turns from the ideal of the priesthood to the harsh realities, not of the world, but of the Church. How can he take on himself the guidance of others in such troubled times—the Church profaned, invective prized, personal rivalries flourishing, all in chaos and confusion? Priests and influential laymen are involved in the strife. Pagans hate us for our dissensions. Our own best people are scandalized. The Christian is even lampooned on the stage. His own disciples make Christ's name to be blasphemed.[4]

Does all of this have a familiar and contemporary ring to it? Gregory is truly dismayed and hesitates to accept the public ministry which his ordination would demand.

> How could I dare to offer to God the external sacrifice, the antitype of the great mysteries, or clothe myself with the garb and name of priest, before my hands had been consecrated by holy works; before my eyes had been accustomed to gaze safely on created things, with wonder only for the Creator, without injury to the creature; before my ear had been sufficiently opened to the instruction of the Lord, and he had

opened my ear to hear without heaviness, and had set a golden ear-ring with precious sardius, that is, a wise man's word in an obedient ear; before my mouth had been opened to draw in the spirit, and opened wide to be filled with the spirit of speaking of wisdom, by divine knowledge, and, as I would add, loosed in due season; before my tongue had been filled with exultation, and become an instrument of divine melody, awaking with glory, awaking right early, and labouring till it cleave to my jaws; before my feet had been set upon the rock, made like hart's feet, and my footsteps directed in a godly fashion so that they should not well-nigh slip, nor slip at all; before all my members had become instruments of righteousness, and all mortality had been put off, and swallowed up of life, and had yielded to the Spirit?[5]

John Chrysostom, as might be expected, also has an exalted view of the ministry of the word and the risks involved. In his work *On the Priesthood* he writes:

Our present inquiry is not about dealings in wheat and barley, or oxen and sheep, or anything else of the kind. It concerns the very Body of Jesus. For the Church of Christ is Christ's own Body, according to St. Paul, and the man who is entrusted with it must train it to perfect health and incredible beauty, by unremitting vigilance to prevent the slightest spot or wrinkle or other blemish of that sort from marring its grace and loveliness. In short, he must make it worthy, as far as lies within human power, of that pure and blessed Head to which it is subjected.[6]

However, John Chrysostom, unlike Gregory Nazianzen, takes a much more positive view. In fact, he seems eager for the battle and indulges in some decidedly military imagery:

We must take great care, therefore, that the word of Christ may dwell in us richly. For our preparation is not against a single kind of attack. This warfare of ours assumes complex forms and is waged by various enemies. They do not all use the same weapons and they have not all trained to attack us in the same manner. Anyone who undertakes to fight them all must know the arts of all. He must be at the same time archer and slinger, cavalry officer and infantry officer, private soldier and general, foot-soldier and hussar, marine and engineer. In military warfare each man is given a particular task and repulses the attacker in that particular way. But in our warfare this is not so. Unless the man who means to win understands every aspect of the art, the devil knows how to introduce his agents at a single neglected spot and so to plunder the flock. But he is baffled when he sees that the shepherd has mastered his whole repertoire and thoroughly understands his tricks.[7]

It is especially in the important ministry of preaching that problems can arise. There is the danger of becoming starved for applause and depressed over the complaints of a demanding congregation:

> For the congregation does not sit in judgment on the sermon as much as on the reputation of the preacher, so that when someone excels everyone else at speaking, then he above all needs painstaking care. He is not allowed sometimes not to succeed—the common experience of all the rest of humanity. On the contrary, unless his sermons always match the great expectations formed of him, he will leave the pulpit the victim of countless jeers and complaints. No one ever takes it into consideration that a fit of depression, pain, anxiety, or in many cases anger, may cloud the clarity of his mind and prevent his productions from coming forth unalloyed; and that in short, being a man, he cannot invariably reach the same standard or always be successful, but will naturally make many mistakes and obviously fall below the standard of his real ability. People are unwilling to allow for any of these factors, as I said, but criticize him as if they were sitting in judgment on an angel.[8]

What is the preacher to do who, because of the ignorance or envy of some listeners, receives little applause and few marks of approval? (In the fourth century, feedback was clearly given; the audience actually applauded and cheered a preaching performance or conspicuously sat on their hands.) Although, as Chrysostom wisely remarks, he knows of no man who does not enjoy praise, the preacher should not strive to be popular.

> So too the man who has accepted the task of teaching should pay no attention to the commendation of outsiders, any more than he should let them cause him dejection. When he has composed his sermons to please God (and let this alone be his rule and standard of good oratory in sermons, not applause or commendation), then if he should be approved by men too, let him not spurn their praise. But if his hearers

do not accord it, let him neither seek it or sorrow for it. It will be
sufficient encouragement for his efforts, and one much better than
anything else, if his conscience tells him that he is organizing and
regulating his teaching to please God. For in fact, if he has already
been overtaken by the desire for unmerited praise, neither his great
efforts nor his powers of speech will be any use. His soul, being
unable to bear the senseless criticisms of the multitude, grows slack
and loses all earnestness about preaching. So a preacher must train
himself above all else to despise praise. For without this addition,
knowledge of the technique of speaking is not enough to ensure
powerful speech.[9]

Chrysostom himself had both natural and acquired skills in public
speaking, and he used them to great effect. But he was wary of the
applause which followed. Jaroslav Pelikan writes:

> As he was moving into the peroration of the seventeenth homily, he
> seems to have been interrupted by applause. "Did ye give praise to what
> hath been said?" he asked. "Nay, I want not applause, nor tumults, nor
> noise. One thing only do I wish, that quietly and intelligently listening,
> you should do what is said. This is the applause, this the panegyric for
> me." He attacked his hearers for treating the liturgy and the sermon as
> though they were a "dramatic spectacle" or a performance to be gawked
> at and cheered but not heeded.[10]

The most famous preacher and bishop in the history of
Constantinople knew as well as anyone how easily a master of words
can create an effect, but the better lesson is the example of one's life.
He studied Christ as an example of a skilled rhetorician to learn how
to adapt his words to his meaning and produce the desired effect in
his listeners, because he felt that the very function of the preacher
was to be the mouthpiece through whom Christ spoke to the people.
Like many preachers, he went to great pains with his sermons; but his
motivation was different from that of most preachers.

> "And if they get applause from the multitude, it is to them as if they
> gained the very kingdom of heaven; but if silence follows the close of
> their speech, it is worse than hell itself, the dejection that falls upon
> their spirits from the silence!" Speaking now of his own feelings as a
> preacher, Chrysostom admitted that it was exhilarating to be
> applauded while he was in the pulpit; but the thrill was brief, for
> afterwards he reflected that many of those who had cheered would not

take the message to heart. The only solution, he announced, was for all applause to be forbidden, and this announcement brought the house down with applause![11]

Although we sometimes lament the difficulty in getting feedback which is honest and helpful for our preaching, the loud and clear Constantinople response obviously was of limited value.

John Chrysostom in the East, so well trained in the art of Demosthenes and Isocrates, and Augustine in Roman Africa, heir of Cicero and Quintilian, may be truly called "giants of the pulpit" in the ancient world. That may not sound like a happy title at the present time when modern pulpit giants have just about become extinct. But the fact is that these men, combining deep faith with the art of the rhetor, were the first masters of sacred eloquence and determined the standards and ideals for Christian preaching for hundreds of years.

GREGORY THE GREAT

Gregory, the abbot of the monastery of St. Andrew at Rome, was another reluctant bishop. He was acclaimed by the people of Rome as their bishop upon the death of Pope Pelagius II in the year 590, but he most sincerely tried to decline the responsibility. When he heard that he was to be pope, he was, he said "so stricken with sorrow that he could hardly speak." The archbishop of Ravenna chided him for his reluctance in a letter. The treatise *Pastoral Care* was the new pope's reply and his apology for attempting to escape the burdensome office.

Since Gregory, and many others, considered the bishop to be the preacher *par excellence*, what he looks for in the episcopal preacher may also be expected in those of lesser rank. He writes:

He, therefore—indeed, he precisely—must devote himself entirely to setting an ideal of living. He must die to all passions of the flesh and by now lead a spiritual life. He must have put aside worldly prosperity; he must fear no adversity, desire only what is interior. He must be a man whose aims are not thwarted by a body out of perfect accord through frailty, nor by any contumacy of the spirit. He is not led to covet the goods of others, but is bounteous in giving of his own. He is quickly moved by a compassionate heart to forgive, yet never so diverted from perfect rectitude as to forgive beyond what is proper. He does no unlawful act himself while deploring those of others, as if they were his own. In the affection of his own heart he sympathizes with the frailties of others, and so rejoices in the good done by his neighbour, as though the progress made were his own. In all that he does he sets an example so inspiring to all others, that in their regard he has no cause to be ashamed of his past. He so studies to live as to be able to water the dry hearts of others with the streams of instruction imparted. By his practice and experience of prayer he has learned already that he can obtain from the Lord what he asks for, as though it were already said to him, in particular, by the voice of experience: *When thou art yet speaking, I will say, "Here I am."* [12]

Gregory is direct and clear when he speaks of the purity in thought required of the pastor:

> No impurity should stain one who has undertaken the duty of cleansing the stains of defilement from the hearts of others as well as from his own. For it is necessary that the hand that aims at cleansing filth should itself be clean, lest, sordid with clinging dirt, it fouls for the worse everything it touches. Wherefore, it is said by the Prophet: *Be ye clean, you that carry the vessels of the Lord.* Those who carry the vessels of the Lord are those who undertake, in reliance on their way of living, to draw the souls of their neighbours to the everlasting holy places. [13]

He warns against loquacity, "a careless and offensive torrent of words," when even what is proper is said in excess or in a slovenly manner. It defiles the speaker himself, inasmuch as it takes no notice of the practical needs of the audience. It would appear that in the sixth century the verbose preacher was also a problem. Gregory does not find him objectionable because he is breaking some rhetorical rule or esthetic maxim, but rather because he is not pastorally attentive to the needs of his flock. They simply do not need a long oration!

For a man who had been a monk for much of his life, he seems fairly open to the idea of the "hyphenated clergyman." The idea of the "worker-priest" is certainly nothing new; in fact, at that time many pastors had a second job. Gregory remarks:

"Secular employments, then, are sometimes to be sympathetically put up with, but never sought after out of affection for them. Otherwise, when they oppress the mind of him who is attached to them, he becomes submerged by the weight and sinks down from the concerns of Heaven even to the very depths."[14]

But he does not hesitate to speak also to those who have the care of souls but would probably prefer to be in a quiet hermitage:

> Some, on the contrary, undertake the charge of the flock, but wish to be so free for spiritual occupations, as not to give any time at all to external matters. Now, when such people wholly neglect to attend to what pertains to the body, they afford no help to their subjects. It is no wonder that their preaching is disregarded for the most part, for while chiding the deeds of sinners, and not giving them the necessities of the present life, their words certainly do not find sympathetic listeners. Doctrine taught does not penetrate the minds of the needy, if a compassionate heart does not commend it to the hearts of hearers; but the seed of the word does germinate promptly, when the kindness of a preacher waters it in the hearer's heart.[15]

He is well aware of the great occupational hazard of every popular preacher, the sin of pride. At the very end of *Pastoral Care*, he spells it out quite vividly:

> Now, seeing that often when a sermon is delivered with due propriety and with a fruitful message, the mind of the speaker is exalted by joy all his own over his performance, he must needs take care to torment himself with painful misgivings: in restoring others to health by healing their wounds, he must not disregard his own health and develop tumours of pride. Let him not, while helping his neighbours, neglect himself, let him not while lifting up others, fall himself. In many instances, indeed, the greatness of certain men's virtues has been an occasion of their perdition, in that they have felt inordinately secure in the assurance of their strength, and they died suddenly because of their negligence. For as virtue struggles against vice, the mind, as it were, exhilarated by this virtue, flatters itself; and it comes to pass that the soul of one actually engaged upon doing good casts aside all anxiety and circumspection, and rests secure in its self-confidence. In this its state of inertia the cunning Seducer enumerates all that the man has done well, and aggrandizes him with conceited thoughts about his pre-eminence over all others. Whence

it happens that in the eyes of the just Judge the consciousness of virtue is a pitfall for the soul. In calling to mind what it has done, in exalting itself before itself, it falls in the presence of the Author of humility.[16]

Gregory's *Pastoral Care* furnished a pattern of conduct for the parish preacher just as the Rule of St. Benedict did for the monks of the West. Leander, Archbishop of Seville, introduced it into all the dioceses of Spain. The Irish monk and missionary, Columban, read it with great delight. And the Benedictine missionary, Augustine, brought Gregory's treatise to England.

The great English scholar, Alcuin, wrote to Eanbald, the Archbishop of York, in 796: "Wherever you go, let the pastoral book of St. Gregory be your companion. Read and re-read it often, that in it you may learn to know yourself and your work, that you may have before your eyes how you ought to live and teach. The book is a mirror of the life of a bishop and a medicine for all the wounds inflicted by the Devil's deception." How many hundreds of preachers of many nationalities felt themselves admonished by Gregory's vigorous words?

> Those who can preach worthily but fear to do so from excessive humility, are to be admonished in one way, and in another, those who are debarred from it by their unfitness or age, and yet are impelled thereto by their hastiness. Men who can preach with good results, but shrink from doing so from inordinate humility, are to be admonished to infer from a consideration of what is a small matter, how greatly they are at fault in matters of greater moment. Thus, if they were to hide from their indigent neighbours money which they themselves have, they would, without doubt, show themselves to be abettors of distress. Let them, then, consider in what great guilt they are implicated, because by withholding the word of preaching from sinning brethren, they are hiding the medicine of life from souls that are dying. . . . If men versed in the medical art were to observe a sore that needed lancing, and yet refused to lance it, surely they would be responsible for a brother's death by their mere failing to act. Let them see, therefore, in what great guilt they are involved who, while recognizing the wounds of the soul, neglect to heal them by the lancet of words.[17]

THE MEDIEVAL VOICES

When the twenty-two-year-old Bernard decided to be a monk, he did not enter Cluny or any of the other established monasteries in

Burgundy. Instead he went to the young, small, very strict, and almost starving community of Citeaux. After only three years, in 1115, he was sent as abbot to begin a new daughter house at Clairvaux. For the rest of his life he was to be the "abbot on the go," responsible for founding seventy more daughter houses (which would produce ninety-four new foundations all over Europe), he would supervise the training of large numbers of monks, and he would preach constantly.

The great basilica of Vezelay still stands on a Burgundian hilltop. There Bernard made the tragic mistake of preaching the Second Crusade. Fortunately, his eloquence and energy were usually used for better purposes. A good example is his work *De Consideratione*.

A Cistercian monk and spiritual son had become pope. Pope Eugene III was soon to receive a treatise from his former abbot in which many subjects are treated. For Bernard, the pontificate is no more than a ministry and the pope is not a sovereign. His charge is stewardship, not rule. The overloaded papal schedule must be corrected so that he can pray and preach. There must be leisure if there is to be papal vitality and wisdom. It would appear that Bernard were speaking not only to Pope Eugene III but to countless busy and harassed pastors in these later days!

Eugene must also know himself and how the human heart behaves. He must understand himself as a sinner and also as one who loves the Lord. He must be aware of ambition and avarice in himself and others. And he must face the paradox of being a man of prayer, a man happy in the study and contemplation of God, and at the same time, a man responsible for an almost unbearable work load. The basic question for Bernard and for Pope Eugene is the conflict between busy responsibility and a deep spiritual commitment to prayer and simplicity of life. The question remains very much *à la page* for most preachers today! There are more than a few pastors who feel that the business of their lives is quite as complicated as that of Pope Eugene, and, while they are not responsible for the regulation of the hierarchy and the protection of the Holy Land, they are accountable for budgets, IRS forms, visitation of the sick, perhaps a school, and who knows what else. Bernard reminds the pope and all of us of our primary concern:

Either deny openly that you are the shepherd of this people or show it by your actions. You will not deny it unless you deny you are the heir of him whose throne you hold. This is Peter, who is known never to have gone in procession adorned with either jewels or silks, covered with gold, carried on a white horse, attended by a knight or surrounded by clamoring servants. But without these trappings, he believed it was enough to be able to fulfill the Lord's command, "If you love me, feed my sheep." In this finery, you are the successor not of Peter, but of Constantine. I suggest that these things must be allowed for the time being, but are not to be assumed as a right. Rather, I urge you on to those things to which I know you have an obligation. You are the heir of the Shepherd and even if you are arrayed in purple and gold, there is no reason for you to abhor your pastoral responsibilities: there is no reason for you to be ashamed of the Gospel. If you but preach the Gospel willingly you will have glory even among the Apostles. To preach the Gospel is to feed. Do the work of an evangelist and you have fulfilled the office of Shepherd. [18]

Toward the end of Book Four, Bernard tells Eugene—and all of us—what every preacher should be. Can we find ourselves in this litany of titles?

You are not the lord of bishops, but one of them, and the brother of those who love God and the companion of those who fear him. For the rest, consider that you ought to be a model of justice, a mirror of holiness, an exemplar of piety, a preacher of truth, a defender of the faith, the teacher of the nations, the leader of Christians, a friend of the Bridegroom, and attendant of the bride, the director of the clergy, the shepherd of the people, the instructor of the foolish, the refuge of the oppressed, the advocate of the poor, the hope of the unfortunate, the protector of orphans, the judge of widows, the eye of the blind, the tongue of the mute, the support of the aged, the avenger of crimes, the terror of evil men, the glory of the good. [19]

Although many authors from the death of Augustine in 430 until the beginning of the twelfth century had exhorted preachers to live a virtuous life and to know the Bible, it was Guibert de Nogent, a Benedictine monk at St. Geremar Abbey, who attempted an organized manual for preachers, the *Liber quo ordine sermo fieri debeat*. He quickly addresses some acute problems:

It is extremely dangerous for a man who has the obligation of preaching ever to stop studying. For just as it is damnable to set an example of vice, so it is almost equally worthy of damnation to refuse to aid sinners through preaching. Individuals have different ideas about preaching, however. Some refuse to do it out of pride, some out of laziness, and some out of envy. Some, I say, despise it because of pride: they see that many preachers display themselves arrogantly and for the sake of vanity, and they wish to avoid the epithet "sermonizers," which describes so contemptible a breed, a class which Gregory Nazianzen called "ventriloquists, because they speak for the belly's sake." They despise all preachers as of this unspeakable type. If a comparison between the two is justified, however, the man who preaches out of a desire for praise does the more good and harms only himself. He at least proclaims to others the teachings they need. The other vilely conceals matter he knows to be useful, and so neither benefits others nor does anything to help himself.

Let us speak, therefore, if we have acquired any knowledge of the sacred pages, as inspired by God, that is, as recognizing that God is the foundation of all that we say. After all, if there is an obligation incumbent upon the instructor of souls, it is that he ought to speak only of God. If he must speak of anything else, then let him treat it as it relates to God and flows from Him as from a special fountain. How great a sacrilege does a man commit when he presumes to seek his own glory in his treatment of things that should tend only to the glory of God. If thievery is the most nefarious action in human relations, what a crime must it not be to steal from God in order to increase ourselves![20]

Guibert combines lofty ideals with some practical and prudent suggestions (which could have come from any numb and abused congregation):

Let the book from which flows the text of our speaking be a pure conscience; in that way, while our tongue announces joy to others, the memory of our own sins will not destroy within and dissipate, with hidden guilt, the force of our speaking. Let a prayer always precede the sermon, so that the soul may burn fervently with divine love; then let it proclaim what it has learned from God so as to inflame the hearts of all hearers with the same interior fire which consumes it. For a tepid sermon, delivered half-heartedly, cannot please even the preacher; wonder of wonders, then, if it should please anyone else. And how can a mangled or stammered phrase serve to inspire others, when we know perfectly well that speech of that kind does not usually soothe the minds of listeners, but rather oppresses them with boredom and seriously irritates and angers them. For this reason,

when we recognize that our intellectual acumen is not at its best and
that what we ought to be saying simply does not come and that the
workings of the mind are under a heavy cloud, then, as I see it, we
know that no real usefulness can result from a sermon drawn out to
great length in these circumstances. After all, if a sermon ought not to
be given at excessive length even when the words come easily and the
fluency is pleasing to the heart, how much less when the memory
fails, the delivery is halting, and the mind is sluggish. As St. Ambrose
said, a tedious sermon arouses anger; and when unrelated topics are
dragged in during the sermon, it usually happens that the hearers lose
everything from the sermon equally, because of their boredom, the
beginning, the conclusion, and everything in between. Where a few
ideas might have been presented effectively, a plethora of ideas
presented at too great length leads to apathy and even, I fear, to
hostility. [21]

Troubles, temptations, and all the many experiences of life can,
according to Guibert de Nogent, be a real help to the preacher:

Anyone having the office of teacher can, if he wishes, be prepared in
every detail, first by knowing himself, and, second, through the lessons
his experience of interior struggles has taught him; this training will be
far richer than anything I could express. In this way the events of his life,
both good and bad, are indelibly imprinted on his memory; because of
them he is able to act wisely for his own salvation and that of others. Any
man, even one without experience, one who has never been part of a
battle, can talk at great length about war, just because he has seen
warriors or heard stories of war; but what a difference there is between
this and the man who can reminisce about war, who has fought or been
besieged, who has gone to war and suffered!
    It is the same in spiritual matters when we hear people speak with
overpowering eloquence about what they have read in books or heard
from others; how greatly they differ from the man who speaks with
real authority of his own spiritual struggles, whose experience is like a
mark to underline what he says, whose personal knowledge is the
witness to the truth of what his mouth speaks. [22]

In the medieval period it was not unusual to write a *Summa* or
compendium. The most famous, of course, is the *Summa
Theologica* of Thomas Aquinas. However, a certain Alan of the Isles
decided to write a *Summa de arte praedicatoria*, that is, A
Compendium on the Art of Preaching. Its preface and forty-eight

chapters cover all the rhetorical aspects of preaching and include sample sermons, even one directed to sleepyheads (*Ad somnolentes*). Some of his strongest words concern the preacher's need for knowledge:

> Preachers need knowledge so that they be experts in both Testaments, discriminating in their analysis of texts, fluent with words, reserved in all their movements, aloof to the world and dedicated to fulfilling their office. Malachi says of the prelate: "The lips of the priest guard knowledge and the people seek instruction from his mouth, for he is a messenger from the Lord of Hosts" (Malachi 2). And Sirach, the son of Jesus, says: "If you have knowledge, answer your neighbour; if not, put your hand on your mouth; do not fall victim to undisciplined speech" (Sirach 5). There is every reason to tremble at the dictum, "If a blind man lead a blind man, both fall into the pit" (Matthew 15: Luke 6). And the Apostle says, "If a man speaks in ignorance, he will be ignored" (I Corinthians 14). And what will the master say to the foolish virgins? "Amen, I say to you, I do not know you" (Matthew 25). Besides, there is the statement, "Cursed is the old man just beginning his education," which is just like "The sinner one hundred years old will be cursed" (Isaiah 65). And there is a deliberately cultivated kind of ignorance, when one could know but refused to learn; this is crass and supine and vincible and therefore inexcusable. Of this it has been written, "He has refused to understand in order that he may do good" (Psalm 34); also, "When a man enjoys honor, he does not understand; he resembles unthinking beasts, he is made like to them" (Psalm 48). This ignorance characterizes those prelates who choose disdainfully to coast along in their blindness; in their pride, they persist in foolishness; they are priests and prophets without reason, teachers of what cannot be, catalogues of things that are not known.
> O vile ignorance! O abominable stupidity! It imposes silence on a prelate, it renders mute the watchdog, the shepherd; it is a frog which, when placed in the dog's mouth, takes away his power to bark. The prelates of our time occupy the chair of the master before they have known the student's bench; they receive the title of teacher before they have worn the gown of the pupil; they would rather stand over than stand with; they prefer the riches of unearned honors to the rewards of dedication. To a prelate of this kind can be directed the admonition, "Physician, heal yourself" (Luke 4); orator, speak to yourself; you are the representative of Christ, imitate his works who "began to do and to teach" (Acts 1). One who teaches without doing contradicts Christ. He imposes unbearable burdens on his subjects

without lifting a finger to help carry the weight. Some hide in a napkin the very talent which divine wisdom has entrusted to them: namely, those who, because of carelessness, refuse to preach. Some hide it in a dungheap: namely, those who contradict their words by their behavior. Some hide it in mud: namely, those who, because of jealousy, hide the word of God.[23]

But there is one voice above all others that we still hear from the Middle Ages. There is one man who, in the minds of many people, has best imitated Jesus in the entire two thousand year history of Christianity. His followers, who form the largest of the religious orders, can be found taking care of the Christian shrines of the Holy Land or runaway teens just off Times Square. For some, of course, Francis of Assisi is merely the sentimental subject for a terra cotta statue to decorate the birdbath in the garden! In fact, he was a man of extraordinary intensity and dedication, both a preacher and a poet, strong and profound.

He had a great respect for the power of the spoken word, and he truly revered preachers. But there can be no doubt that for St. Francis the most potent sermon was preached by good example. He once told one of his brothers to walk though the crowded street of a town; it was not necessary for him to say a word, for the gospel was preached by the obvious humility and poverty of the man. Even the other brothers who preached through their words were, above all, to be men of prayer. He insisted: "A preacher ought first in secret prayer to draw the water he intends later to pour out in sacred sermon; he ought to grow warm within before he utters cold words without."[24]

Together with Dominic, who founded his Order of Preachers about the same time, Francis knew that preaching was neglected in many places. He sent out his friars to bring the gospel to the poor in the villages and towns of Umbria and Tuscany and, later, to far distant places. But always there was to be obedience to authority; he ordered:

None of the brothers shall preach contrary to the procedure and doctrine of the holy Roman Church, and unless the license has been granted him by his minister. The minister in turn shall be on his guard not to grant any the license inadvisedly. All the brothers, however, shall preach by their actions. And let no minister or

preacher seize on the ministry of the brothers or the office of preaching as his right, but at any point of time it is enjoined on him let him give up his office without remonstrating.
For that reason, in the charity which is God (cf. I Jn. 4, 8) I beseech all my brothers whether clerical or lay, whether engaged in preaching or in prayer or in labor, to aim at keeping humble in everything; not to boast, nor be pleased with themselves nor interiorly elated, at the good words or deeds, or in fine anything good, which God says or does or accomplishes in them or through them at times, in keeping with what our Lord says, "But rejoice not at this that the spirits are subject to you" (Lk. 10, 20). Let us know for certain that nothing but our vices and sins belong to us. And we ought to be the happier if we fall into various trials (Jas. 1, 2) and when we are enduring all sorts of distress and hardship of body and soul in this world for the sake of life everlasting.
So, brothers, let us all be on our guard against any pride and vainglory. Let us keep ourselves free of the wisdom of this world and the prudence of the flesh; for it is the spirit of the flesh to want and strive hard at making words but little at accomplishing, and it is not bent on the inner religious virtue and holiness of the spirit, but wants and craves the religious virtue and holiness that shows outwardly to people. It is of such that our Lord says, "Amen I say to you, they have received their reward" (Matt. 6:2).[25]

In 1221, Francis resigned as minister general of the Friars Minor and frankly wondered whether he should go out into the world at all and continue preaching or rather spend his time in prayer for the ends he had in view. With great simplicity he asked:

Brothers, what do you advise and commend? That I give myself wholly to prayer, or that I go about and preach?
For of course as an insignificant, unlettered person without skill in speech I have received the grace of prayer rather than that of speech. Then too in prayer one seems to win and heap up graces whereas in preaching one as it were distributes the gifts received from Heaven. In prayer there is purification of the interior affections and union with the one true and sovereign Good together with invigoration of virtue; in preaching our spiritual feet pick up dust, we are distracted in many ways, and discipline suffers relaxation. Finally in prayer we address and listen to God, and associate with the angels as if leading an angelic life; in preaching we have to exercise much condescension toward the people and in living among them as people do, we have to think and see and speak and hear things that are human.

On the other hand, there is one thing that seems to outweigh all this before God, the supreme Wisdom, descended from the bosom of the Father for the salvation of souls in order to instruct the world by his example and speak the word of salvation to the people, whom he was both to redeem with the price and cleanse with the bath and nourish with the drink of his sacred Blood, keeping nothing whatever back for himself that he did not give away liberally for our salvation. And since we ought to do everything according to the model of what we see in him as on a high mountain, it seems to be more pleasing to God for me to interrupt my retirement and go out for such work.[26]

And so Francis settled his doubt in favor of preaching. He continued to speak to the people wherever he went until, blind and dying, he asked to be carried down from the hilltop town of Assisi to the little chapel of St. Mary of the Angels. Francis, the poet and mystic, understood the powerful language of symbol, and he asked to be allowed to lie on the ground and die in utter poverty as the brothers sang Psalm 141 and his own Canticle of Brother Sun. The last stanza is this:

Be praised, my Lord, through our Brother Death of Body,
From whom no man among the living can escape.
Woe to those who in mortal sins will die:
Blessed those whom he will find in your most holy graces,
For the second death will do no harm to them.
Praise and bless my Lord, and thank him too,
And serve him all, in great humility.[27]

Although scores of Augustine's and John Chrysostom's sermons have been preserved, only fragments of Francis' oral legacy remain. Unlike them, Francis knew nothing of rhetorical rules and classical models. But it is certainly *Il Poverello* which continues to have the greatest influence on later generations. It is true that the Christmas sermon he preached at Greccio in 1223 showed him to be a master of nonverbal communication. In the Michaelmas fast of 1224 on the heights of Mount La Verna he received the Stigmata. But more than these extraordinary moments, it was the whole tone of Francis' life that makes him such a memorable herald of the gospel. Has there been, since the apostolic age, anyone who better understood the link between poverty, prayer, and preaching?

For Francis, his whole life became a sermon or song of love. Perhaps his spirit is well presented in this little story from the *Fioretti* (in a quaint but delightful English translation):

When as Saint Francis was going one day from Perugia to Saint Mary of the Angels with Brother Leo in the spring tide, and the very bitter cold grievously tormented him, he called to Brother Leo that was going on before and said thus: "Brother Leo, though the Brothers Minor throughout all the world were great examples of sanctity and true edifying, nathless write it down and take heed diligently that not therein is perfect joy." And going on a little further, Saint Francis called a second time: "O Brother Leo, albeit the Brother Minor should give sight to the blind, make straight the the crooked, cast out devils, make the deaf to hear, the lame to walk, the dumb to speak, and (greater still) should raise them that have been dead for four days' space, write that not herein is perfect joy." And going on a little, he cried aloud: "O Brother Leo, if the Brother Minor should know all tongues and all sciences and all the Scriptures, so that he could prophesy and reveal not only things to come but also the secrets of consciences and souls, write that not therein is perfect joy." Going on yet a little further, Saint Francis called aloud once more: "O Brother Leo, thou little sheep of God, albeit the Brother Minor should speak with the tongue of angels, and know the courses of the stars and the virtues of herbs; and though all the treasures of the earth were revealed unto him and he understood the virtues of birds, and of fishes, and of all animals, and of men, and of trees, and of stones, and of roots, and of waters, write that not therein is perfect joy." And going on a little further, Saint Francis cried aloud: "O Brother Leo, albeit the Brother Minor could preach so well as to turn all the infidels to the faith of Christ, write that not therein is perfect joy." And this manner of speech continuing for full two miles, Brother Leo with much marvel besought him, saying: "Father, I pray thee in the name of God that thou tell me, wherein is perfect joy." And Saint Francis thus made answer: "When we come to Saint Mary of the Angels, all soaked as we are with rain and numbed with cold and besmirched with mud and tormented with hunger, and knock at the door; and the porter comes in anger and says: 'Who are you?' and we say: 'We be two of your brethren'; and he says, 'Ye be no true men; nay, ye be two rogues that gad about deceiving the world and robbing the alms of the poor; get ye gone' and thereat he shuts to the door and makes us stand without in the snow and the rain, cold and a-hungered, till nightfall; if therewithal we patiently endure such wrong and such cruelty and such rebuffs without being disquieted and without murmuring against him; and with humbleness and charity bethink us that this porter knows us full well and that God makes him to speak against us; O Brother Leo, write that herein is perfect joy. And if we be instant in knocking and he come out full of wrath and drive us away as importunate knaves, with insults and buffetings, saying: 'Get ye gone hence, vilest of thieves, begone to the alms-house, for here ye shall find nor food nor lodging'; if we suffer this with patience and with gladness and with love, O Brother Leo, write that herein is perfect joy. And if we still constrained by hunger, cold and night, knock yet again and shout and with much weeping pray him for the love of God that he will but open and let us in; and he yet more enraged should say: 'These be importunate knaves, I will pay them well as they deserve,' and should rush out with a knotty stick and taking us by the hood, throw us upon the ground and send us rolling in the snow and beat us with all the knots of that stick: if with patience and with gladness we suffer all these things, thinking on the pains of the blessed Christ, the which we ought to suffer for the love of Him; O Brother Leo, write that here and herein is perfect joy: then hear the conclusion of the whole matter, Brother Leo: Above all graces and gifts of the Holy Spirit, that Christ granteth to His beloved, is to overcome oneself, and willingly for the love of Christ endure pains and insults and shame and want: inasmuch as in all other gifts of God we may not glory, since they are not ours but God's; Whence saith the Apostle: What hast thou that thou hast not received of God? And if thou has received it of Him, wherefore boastest thou thyself as if thou hadst it of thyself? But in the cross of tribulation and affliction we may boast, since this is ours; and therefore saith the Apostle, I would not that I should glory save in the cross of our Lord Jesus Christ."[28]

However quaint, however removed from our technological society, the voices of the pioneers speak loud and clear to us of the preacher's identity in Jesus Christ. The centuries which followed would certainly yield even more examples, and so would preachers of this century, this decade. But these particular voices prepare us uniquely for the next steps in our quest to understand the person in the pulpit.

III. "WHEN YOU CARE ENOUGH . . . "

Secular subjects have long had an important place in the formation of the clergy. For centuries philosophy was considered an absolute prerequisite for the study of theology and for the proper training of a preacher. It has only been in recent years, when philosophy departments have become an intellectual smorgasbord offering a bewildering array of contradictory systems, that theology faculties realized that their students were suffering from an indigestion of the mind. Some theology professors would now prefer students uncontaminated by a mix of Marx, Sartre, Wittgenstein, and Aristotle!

Sociology has also had its day, and at the moment anthropology seems to be popular. But, above all, it is psychology that has been the most powerful of the secular subjects to touch the training and life of the contemporary preacher.

The magic names of Freud, Adler, Jung, Rogers, Frankl, and Fromm are heard in the seminary as well as on the university campus. Psychologists have joined seminary faculties both to teach courses in abnormal behavior and to administer tests which help to screen out the more bizarre applicants. Psychiatrists have been named as seminary consultants to examine formational programs and, when necessary, to treat seminarians who manifest some dysfunctional behavior. More than a few seminarians have wondered if the twelve apostles would have gotten through the testing and the interviews which they must endure!

Although much of the original fervor is gone and psychology is no longer seen as a cure-all for the problems of the modern seminary or the ministry, the psychological influence remains in required clinical pastoral education programs, courses in group dynamics, and sensitivity training. And, of course, there is a residue of jargon as ministers continue to strive to "get in touch with themselves."

But, should it become fashionable to minimize the contribution of philosophy and psychology in the formation of the preacher, something important will have been forgotten. For grace builds on nature. One must be a good human being before one can be a good Christian and a good minister of the gospel. Anything which contributes to a better understanding of what it means to be human is valuable for those who are called to preach. Although there are many important trends in psychology and philosophy, varied opinions, and valuable insights, I would like in our limited space to look at the concept of caring and examine its implications for the preacher.

To care for another is at the center of the ministerial life. As Milton Mayerhoff has said:

> In the context of a man's life, caring has a way of ordering his other values and activities around it. When this ordering is comprehensive, because of the inclusiveness of his caring, there is a basic stability in his life; he is "in place" in the world, instead of being out of place, or merely drifting or endlessly seeking his place. Through caring for certain others, by serving them through caring, a man lives the meaning of his own life. In the sense in which a man can ever be said to be at home in the world, he is at home not through dominating, or explaining or appreciating, but through caring and being cared for. [1]

Let us explore Mayerhoff's insights and their relevance for us. What does caring tell us about the character of the preacher?

The person who cares for another does not want to dominate and control the other; there is not a need to possess and use the other to satisfy personal needs. The father who cares for his son feels that the child has value in his own right and is worth something quite apart from what he is able to do for him. The child has been given as a trust; there is caring but not manipulating.

A father is conscious that his son needs him in order to grow, but he also knows that the individuality of his son is not to be crushed. The response of the father is determined by his son's needs, and he is guided in his caring by following the boy's growth with respect. So it is with the good preacher. The congregation is not "owned" by the minister. Its needs and the direction of its growth will determine how the minister prepares a sermon.

However, as Mayerhoff remarks, "Direction that comes from the growth of the other should not be confused with being 'other directed,' where this refers to the kind of conformity in which I lose touch with both myself and the other."[2] The paradox is this, that the more I am absorbed as a preacher in the needs of my listeners, the more I am responsive to the gospel and to myself. When I experience the worth of the other, the importance and value of my congregation, I find myself more sensitive concerning my message and my own worth.

Caring means devotion. Just as friendship is not like instant coffee but rather grows slowly, emerging from a relationship as persons go deeper and become more trusting, so also the preacher who cares grows in devotion to his flock. There is no caring without devotion. The devoted preacher stays with his or her people even when there are grave difficulties and many compelling reasons to abandon them. Like a mother who cares for her child in an illness, there is no sense that the parental obligations of getting up at night, sitting by the bed, cancelling the party or the shopping outing to remain present to the child are heavy burdens. The preacher who is devoted to the congregation and wants it to be healthy and strong in the Lord experiences the obligations of prayer, preparation, and preaching as things that he or she wants to do. The congregation becomes an extension of the preacher and is experienced as such, just as the mother experiences her child as an extension of herself. The happiness and well-being of the preacher are bound up with the happiness and health of the congregation and whatever is necessary to foster what is good for the flock is done without complaint and indeed intensely desired by the pastor. What strangers would consider obstacles, or at least irritations, are taken in stride. Devotion involves persistence and generous giving even when the difficulties of the situation would persuade one to hold back or to give up.

The caring preacher wants his or her parishioners to grow, to move from immaturity to maturity, to go from a kind of spiritual childishness to the wisdom and strength of Christian adults. What does this mean? The preacher who cares wants to assist in producing parishioners who care. One is growing when one is starting to care for someone who is not oneself. When a child begins to care for a puppy or a kitten, there is already a sign of growth. When, after a few years perhaps, the child shows concern about the welfare of a schoolmate, there is further evidence that growth is taking place. The teenage girl who is deeply distressed because of her boyfriend's drinking and what it is doing to his life may be worried for herself, but primarily she is caring for someone apart from herself. The caring pastor wants a congregation which also cares. The ultimate success of a Christian life is measured by the extent of our caring. "Whatsoever you do to the least of my people, that you do unto me."

But we cannot care unless we know. We may have some general idea about needy people in some far-distant and little-known country, but, if we know almost nothing about them, can we muster anything more than some good intentions? Yet vague and sentimental regard is not proper caring. If we say about God, "to know Him is to love Him," then as preachers we can also say that we will respond properly to our people and indeed love them only when we discover who they are. When we learn about their good points and their weaknesses, and when we recognize them with their unique qualities as having worth, then caring for them becomes possible.

It follows, of course, that the preacher must make the effort to know. He or she must take the time to talk with, to question, to listen carefully to the people. The preacher's ears and heart must be open to the members of the parish as they are open to the Lord. It is not necessary that the preacher be able to do a sociological report on the parish. Parents know their children but would find it difficult or impossible to articulate what they know. Good pastors may be quite incapable of verbalizing all that they know about the flock committed to their care; yet, each member of the flock is known as an individual and appreciated as someone special and unique.

It has been said that truly hearing and reacting to feedback makes the difference between success and failure. In sports or the arts or social life, it would seem the successful person is the one who learns from and does not replicate mistakes, but repeats and perhaps improves on what appears to work. In any case, the person who cares must always be alert to what happens as a result of his or her actions. The preacher wants to find out what resulted from his or her words. Should those words be repeated or changed? Or should there be instead a period of waiting and silence? What modifications are called for in delivery and content?

The caring preacher is not rushed or frenzied. Athough he or she has a sense of the urgency of the gospel and may be well aware of the inexorable and swift passing of time, he or she knows that growth cannot be forced on a congregation. The Holy Spirit breathes where and when it wills. A child cannot be rushed into adolescence; a Christian cannot be dragged into full maturity in Christ. There is a need for time and space, for a gentle patience. The patience of the preacher is not a stepping back from the people, a cool indifference which deigns to tolerate their slowness and their foibles. Rather, it means entering more closely into the lives of the people and learning that growth, especially Christian growth, is not easily programmed. We come to find that, since we are neither robots nor angels, our minds are often clouded and our wills vacillating. We arc victims of doubt and confusion; I must be patient with them and with myself.

As a preacher, I am not allowed a distorted view of my people or myself. I might like, for example, to see them as intellectuals and myself as a Harvard chaplain. In fact, most of them work in the mills, and I am of definitely limited genius! Or, I would like them to be young and liberal, when in reality the majority are senior citizens and staunch Republicans. I may have a pastoral vision of how charitable and generous, instructed and devout, socially conscious and hungry for justice my people may become in the future (after a few years of listening to me on Sunday?)—but what are they like right now? What are the facts about my parish? I must see the situation as it is, no better and no worse. And, probably even more painful, I must see myself as I am, not pretending I am more wise, zealous, dedicated, and hopeful than I really am. But also not pretending I am less so! In a word, I must be honest to be a caring preacher.

Why did I decide to follow this vocation? Why am I preparing this particular sermon for this Sunday and these people? In what am I truly interested? What are my pet projects, my favorite ideas, the ideals to which I cling, the things I would take with me to a desert island? There is little doubt that my motivation is mixed in my ministerial life, but dare I estimate the percentage of selfishness in the mixture? How much for the greater glory of God, and how much for me?

To be honest does not mean coming up with consoling or even correct answers for these and similar questions, but it does mean asking them in simplicity and tranquility. It does mean learning from the answers and making the changes that seem indicated.

THE TRUSTING PREACHER

How many pastors really do not have confidence in their people? Perhaps their attitude is based on a theology; they would agree with Augustine when he spoke about the *massa damnata* or with the Jansenists on the "very small number of the elect." The majority of the flock look like unruly sheep who are not to be trusted. They must be whipped into line by strong language; the ideas which they produce are suspect and unworthy. They must be indoctrinated and given no opportunity to comment. Their questions are ruled impertinent and out-of-order.

A lack of trust which is openly or subtly communicated teaches the listeners not to trust themselves to risk or to grow. The parent who will not allow the child to ride on a bicycle because of a possible fall shows a fearfulness and lack of courage. The pastor who distrusts the people preaches in an authoritarian and paternalistic way and tries to dominate in order to exclude any chance of a mistake or an accident. Everything must be sure and safe. He or she may boast of fidelity to the gospel, but, in fact, the real needs of the flock are forgotten and the needs of the preacher have become primary.

The preacher who proclaims love for the congregation and then seeks to "protect" it by making it dependent on obedience to his or her words is like the parent who fears an independent child and keeps control by overprotecting and discouraging independence and maturity.

It would seem to be an occupational hazard of the clergy to develop a "Messiah complex." Preachers become saviors. The foolish Christians in their care will go to hell unless their force, energy, and skill snatches them from the hand of Satan. It is, of course, a completely heterodox position and, intellectually, most preachers would recognize it as such. However, in practice, it guides the lives of not a few.

It is Jesus Christ who does the saving, and the people in (or out) of the pews are, first of all, his. It is Jesus Christ who has deigned to allow us into his service to speak the gospel words, but while we may be useful to him, none of us is indispensible. The ultimate trust of both preacher and people must be in the Lord.

If I am truly to care for my congregation, I must also trust myself. Knowing that I can and do make mistakes, I must be confident that my future words and actions will be better. Knowing that I have had proper training, have proven abilities, have a call to this ministry, and have prayed for help, I must now speak about what is important and relevant for the Christian people. Constant indecision, scrupulousness, and fearfulness indicate that I am thinking too much about myself. I do not trust God or the strength which he has given me.

The caring preacher learns from the congregation just as any good professor learns from the students. And, of course, this involves true humility. But if there is an honest desire to help in the growth of the parishioners, then certainly an attitude of omniscience is out of place. As Mayerhoff rightly remarks, "There is a sense in which the man who cares basically begins anew regardless of how extensive his previous experience has been, for the problem is always one of appropriateness to this novel situation, and this situation is, generally speaking, not simply a repetition of the past requiring only a mechanical application of principles."[3]

How many times has a pastor been moved from one parish to another and thought he could give the same old sermons from the new pulpit? They had been successful in one place, so they should also work in the new location. It is easier to use a tested formula than to learn from the new congregation.

Or there's the eager young preacher who charges out of the seminary, sure that he is God's gift to a benighted people, and gives sermons prepared for a homiletics class or in slavish imitation of some academic model. (I remember giving a grammar school graduation sermon based on the exalted thoughts of a famous theologian! Needless to say, it was a disaster!) In our arrogance, do we really care about the needs and sensibilities of the folk, or rather are we preoccupied with our reputation for profundity or charm? Humble learning is necessary. And the people are our instructors.

We grow with our people. We are not the same on our tenth or twentieth anniversaries as we were on the day of our ordination. Part of the reason is that the people we have worked with have formed us. Our first assignment is, of course, especially important. We are most open to learning and growing at that time. However, even after many years of ministry, we still need our people at least as much as they need us. By caring for them we become more what we should be. It is a strange and sad situation to be a preacher without people, a shepherd who has no sheep or lambs. Preachers need people.

THE COMPETENT PREACHER

When we really care for the people, we want to have those skills which will help them to grow. Caring is more than just wanting to help, having goodwill and generous desires. It leads us to take those steps which will make us capable of helping, of doing what we are supposed to do. For preachers, it means training, practice, preparation in various ways, a seriousness about our function, an appreciation of our calling, and an attention to our own religious life. How much do we really care about these particular people? What are we willing to do for them? These are basic questions, but much depends on the answers which we give.

Most preachers are sent to a particular flock, and this is a good thing. We must know our sheep, and they should come to recognize our voice. Ours is not a casual commitment but an on-going ministry. Pastors are rightly wary of wandering preachers who come in for a "one shot" performance. They do not know the people; they do not understand their special joys and sorrows and needs; they are not going to be involved in their lives. How can they love them? How can they truly care?

For caring would seem to demand stability. Yet it is a lack of continuity which marks many congregations today and makes good preaching and Christian growth so very difficult. In the suburbs young executives come and go at the will of their companies, dragging a wife, kids, and furniture from Boston to San Diego to Kansas City. In the city there is rapid turnover among young singles and families; 50 percent or more may be new faces each year. The clergy too are transferred rather too frequently. How is it possible to have the feelings of loyalty and security which our grandparents had about their parishes? With the people in the pew and the people at the pulpit being replaced so rapidly, caring does become especially difficult. There is little chance for trust and friendship between preacher and people in a mobile and rootless society.

Over much of this mobility we have little control. Nevertheless, we must do what we can to minimize its unhappy effects. Pastors, at least, should stay with one flock long enough for some sense of continuity to develop. There may be traveling preachers who move from town to town and from church to church. And there will be apostles of the mass media who speak to the faceless and generally silent millions out there in television land. But above all, a Christian community must experience a pastor who is constant and who is committed to help it grow in the way of the Gospel in season and out of season.

If we who preach understand our own need for the gospel, our own need to grow as Christians in an ongoing conversion of mind and heart, then we will be able to respond to the religious needs of the people we care for. It is not that we must experience everything that each person in the congregation has experienced. There are too many variables. We are not to pretend that differences in age, sex, background, and personality do not exist. We are not in exactly the same "world" as another. But we can see that "world" and, as Jesus himself did, we can walk into it in order to be with the one who lives there.

The pages of the four Gospels are full of people who no longer felt alone because this wonderful and loving "son of the carpenter" had come into their world and had learned what it was like to be a fisherman, a widow, a father whose daughter had died, a detested tax collector, a prostitute, a blind man, and a much-divorced Samaritan woman. Jesus was only in his early thirties; he had no children and was not even married. But men and women, old and young, were able to open themselves up to him and to be helped. They felt very quickly that they did not have to conceal themselves because Jesus had come into their various "worlds" not to pass judgment on them but to care for them, to help them.

Jesus did not merely have information about people. He had not simply "studied" them to collect data and perhaps use them as "case studies" or colorful examples. He was not an investigative reporter, a sociologist, an anthropologist, or a psychologist. He cared nothing for professional fees or a vita full of publications. He did not use people or remain content to know them from the outside. Rather he was with them in their world. And he was willing to pay the price necessary to enter their world, a price in time, effort, energy, and humility.

We can only imagine the expression on the face of Jesus or the look in his eyes when he found people ready to leave their past and begin to grow in the new life which he offered. Because he cared for them, he was happy to see their growth; and his happiness, in whatever way he expressed it, gave them courage to go further, to have still greater trust and to appreciate their own nobility.

People truly trusted Jesus and opened their hearts to him. They were willing to show their wounds. Because they knew that Jesus was for them, a caring person, they revealed the pain which was in them and healing followed. But Jesus did not make decisions for them; he was never condescending. He did not come to lead people back into immaturity but to bring them a new freedom. And that included the freedom to take responsibility for the decisions of a lifetime.

Because Jesus cared so much for his people many questions which might well have interested someone of his intelligence and occupied a good amount of time appear to be of little importance. Politics, income, position, family, housing, food and clothes, intricate religious questions, secular art and literature—all of these things are either ignored or at least take a decidedly secondary place. It is not that Jesus denied the validity of these concerns for many people. It was just that, for him, they seemed significant only if they touched upon the welfare of those he cared for.

Could it be that the uneasy feelings of so many clergy that their lives are artificial and vaguely disordered and that their hearts as well as their ministries are fragmented and undisciplined are caused by a thin and anemic caring? In contrast with the fruitful caring of Jesus, so full of patient devotion, humility, and honesty, our caring for the people remains a secondary concern in our busy lives. We may be busy with ideas and activity, but there is no center for an integration of our thoughts and actions. In some sense, our ministry remains a kind of diversion and the needs of our people a bit of an intrusion. We resent asceticism, or the giving up of values and experiences, which Jesus accepted so willingly, because for us caring is not primary. We harbor a lingering anger because of the time and sweat we must spend for our ministerial work and seek frequent compensation in recreation. But even our leisure may be tainted by guilt and discontent. We are distracted and perplexed by minor problems; we become anxious and alienated. Although we cannot really be described as hirelings (for surely our ideals and motives are better than that!) yet we are something less than caring shepherds. We are estranged and confused.

Clearly we must care about ourselves. We must appreciate that we also have needs for growth. In fact, if we are unable to care for ourselves, is it even possible to care for others? In addition, we will have others to care for besides the people in the congregation. We all have families and friends. But there must be a priority, a compatibility, and a harmony among the carings in our lives. However, do I see people committed to my care as primary, so that "in conjunction with other carings, they have become a center around which my life can be significantly ordered?"[4]

We have all read the New Testament. We know well enough what is asked of Christians, and we have quite a good idea of what the Lord wants to find in those who would preach his message. These are ideals. We profess them, but it is the continuing process of caring that makes them actual for us and helps them to live in us. We then discover the nobility of our calling and the meaning of our lives as Christian preachers. We begin to understand what it means to be a shepherd when we start to be aware of being needed by the flock. This has nothing to do with receiving from the flock a warm regard and words of appreciation and thanks. There are many who are frankly unable to find or express such words. Poor and uneducated people, for example, may seldom invite the minister to supper and tell him how good he is. The rich, on the other hand, may frequently have the minister as a dinner guest, but, what is even more devastating, may let it be known that they really don't need him!

But, as much as we would like to hear from them all the words that would strengthen and console us in our labors, we may have to forego that delight and simply and honestly remember that we have been called to care. The poor or the rich have been entrusted to us. They will not understand unless some person shows them. The faith of all depends on hearing. Neither rich nor poor are called into a Christian community and nourished there without the preaching of someone who cares. As preachers, therefore, we very much belong in the Christian view of life, and in this world, we become aware of our worth.

And so we are less concerned with the gratitude that is shown to us and more interested in the ways we can show our gratitude. For we are grateful to God who has called and sustained us and to our congregation which has instructed and challenged us. Perhaps we best show our thanks by still more generous and honest caring.

Clearly, a life of caring is not without its sorrow and frustrations. Caring will help integrate our life, but it does not make it comfortable. There are probably safer paths for avoiding hardship and gaining more abundant pleasures. But when we know that it is our calling to be pastors, and that the pastor is one who cares in a special way for a given group of people, we do see with greater clarity the pattern of our lives. Labor and self-denial, prayer and penitence do not become easy, but are more profoundly understood as necessary.

Moreover, when we understand our preaching as a pastoral and caring expression, indeed the first and most important of pastoral tasks and the deepest manifestation of our caring, a simplification takes place in our lives. There can be a wonderful elimination of spiritual and material clutter and a new, peaceful, and joyful concentration on what is relevant.

A parent, a doctor, or a teacher who deeply cares does not live free of pain. But none of them would really want to change places with someone else. The preacher who allows a deep and devoted caring to take over in his or her heart, who becomes truly interested in a community of people and learns from them their needs and hopes, and who rejoices in their growth in the life of Jesus, will no longer be restless and fragmented, no longer anxious about being somewhere else doing something else.

The title of this chapter should not be completed: "When you care enough to preach your very best," but rather: "When you care enough, *you do* preach your very best." And, thanks be to God, you are happy doing it!

IV. THAT SPECIAL SPARKLE

A friend of mine, working in a rather large Chicago Catholic parish, was describing his preaching schedule for the last week: "I preached twice on Sunday morning at the nine and ten-thirty masses. Of course in our parish the people expect a short homily at all the daily masses too. Then there were two funerals, and on Saturday there was a wedding. On Tuesday night the high school graduates had a reunion preceded by a liturgy in the chapel; they asked me to preach. On Wednesday we had an ecumenical service in the Methodist church, and I was the preacher. On Friday afternoon we had a liturgy for the eighth graders right in their classroom, and so I had to talk. At least this week we didn't have any baptisms, reconciliation services, public anointing of the sick, or confirmations!"

If my arithmetic is correct, this man preached—not counting the short daily homilies—on eight different occasions. The Sunday morning homily, of course, was given twice. At all the other times he was expected to preach a fresh sermon! And many would testify that such a preaching workload in many parishes is not at all extraordinary.

How many people in the communications business are faced with anything like it? The actor repeats the same lines every night. The television newscaster takes his material from the wire services, has the help of other writers, and then reads his comments from the prompter. A politician working to get reelected usually has professional writers and then repeats his address before various audiences. The nightclub comic may ad lib for a time but often repeats his gags. It is only the pastor who is expected to be creative, producing fresh and significant material about the most important subject that anyone can deal with, and then personally present it in a lively and interesting oral style and do this not once but seven or eight times each week!

As might be expected, ideas, examples, and stories will be repeated at different weddings and funerals after a time. Yet, for a preacher to succumb to a routine and to begin grinding out a stock sermon for such important occasions is deadly for all concerned. There is a need for a fresh approach, a personal reference, that touch of newness which the good news should always have. And even in the small rural community where the preacher gives one sermon each Sunday, the people know that talk about God and the world, sin and salvation, virtue and vice, must not sound stale. Certainly the topics which we speak about are not to be dismissed frivolously. It is expected therefore that the words which we use will command attention and maintain interest. For many consider that the unpardonable sin is to bore people with the gospel of our Lord Jesus Christ.

All of this means, of course, that the much ignored, maligned, and suspicious faculty called imagination is a high priority item for the preacher. After the all-important personal holiness and understanding of the Christian message must come an abundant creativity, the result of a lively imagination. That precious spark, so cherished by poets and artists and inventors, is also the treasure of the preacher who wants to be more than a weary hack.

Many teachers today feel that a child's imagination, obviously full of life during kindergarten and the early grades, is trampled on during junior high school. As education proceeds, imagination seems to wither. Almost all of our schooling, at least in the western world, tends to train us in logical thinking. The child is taught not to make mistakes. The prize goes to the one who excels in logicial thinking, who is reasonable and predictable, and who can sift and analyze data. Reason and judgment grow, but creativity is allowed to dwindle. Many seem to become ashamed of their imagination and consider it childish. It is allowed out of the closet only for the trivial moments of life.

Several studies have confirmed that imagination contracts as knowledge and judgment expand. It would seem to follow that as knowledge expands in the university or seminary in the struggle for an advanced degree, the imaginative spark wanes still further. Higher education, well organized to sharpen the critical faculty, seldom encourages a flight of fancy! The American clergy are, for the most part, the products of a system which features logic, criticism, and hard-nosed perfectionism. Granted that these are values, they do not, however, help form preachers who are comfortable with their imaginations.

THE IMAGINATIVE PREACHER

Although many argued with Albert Einstein's dictum that "imagination is more important than knowledge," it is difficult to admit that it is any less important for a preacher today. Whatever can be done to foster its growth and its sparkle in seminarians or in ordained preachers should be encouraged. Recently, however, the situation has become more difficult. Formerly, students who began theological studies had behind them a solid background in the liberal arts. Although it would be naive to think that the so-called liberal arts were always taught in a liberal way, still there was an exposure to Cicero and Plato, to Shakespeare and Dickens, to Robert Frost and T. S. Eliot. Being forced to work with the declensions and conjugations of Latin and Greek grammar brought an appreciation of English grammar. Reading history gave a feeling for the follies, the tragedies, and the hopes of the human race. Music worked its special magic not only in the classroom but also in glee clubs and school choirs and orchestras. A dramatic sense and self-confidence were both developed by taking part in Gilbert and Sullivan operettas, oral interpretation programs, and all manner of plays. A class on the art of Michelangelo was followed by a class on the art of big city politics in the twentieth century. A student might finish dissecting a cat in biology class in time to finish a paper on the comedies of Aristophanes. Almost everyone got a taste of physics, chemistry, math, and some modern language. There were many oral presentations and many, many papers. These, of course, were carefully corrected (usually in red ink with eight points off for misspelling!) and returned with a grade to the curious student.

The idea was, of course, that, being involved in the sciences and arts, and learning of the imaginative flashes which had resulted in giant leaps forward in medicine or physics, or in works of great splendor in architecture or painting, the student would obtain a wideness and depth of vision. Some of the wit and wisdom of the "great ones" would rub off on a new generation. Needless to say, it did not always work; probably it did not usually work. But, now and again, this richness and variety did provide a stimulus for a nascent creativity. It helped a new generation to understand at least some of its roots. The liberal arts did what they were supposed to do, namely, liberate the human spirit to live more fully, to think and to do something noble and beautiful and good.

The liberal arts are not substitutes for imagination, but rather provide a wonderful series of houses through which it can roam and grow. Unfortunately, today the seminary student or young pastor may have had only an extremely truncated version of all of this or, to put it most kindly, a completely "non-traditional" background. It is not that a background in supermarket or playground administration does not supply certain skills; however, it has limited value for a man or woman who must be constantly creative with words and images.

Just as remedial reading is sometimes necessary in high school, "remedial arts" will be necessary to help the imaginative preacher. Something can be done for men and women who have been denied, usually through no fault of their own, a meeting with Chaucer and Cervantes, Goethe and Tolstoy, Molière and Dante. Without denying the value of courses and books to help the modern pastor *know* more, may we suggest that the present communication crisis in the Christian church indicates a more urgent need. What can be done to help the preacher be imaginative, to see, to feel, to speak? What help is possible for the pastor who must *create*?

Our imaginations need all the help that they can get—and from the very best sources! The ability to visualize, to foresee, and to generate ideas is a gift given by God, but in many highly educated clergy it has not been honored and has been allowed to atrophy. But it can be warmed and revived by being brought close to the great creative works of other people. When enough sparks from the imaginative fires of others are brought close to us, there is a very good chance that our own cold imagination will also catch fire once again.

It is not, of course, only the masterpieces of the past which can provide a life-restoring warmth for a cold and damp imagination. Horace and Ovid, Euripides and Sophocles—they will always be rediscovered by a new generation when it comes to agree with Horace that the purpose of literature is both *docere* and *placere*. The great classics (at least in a good English translation) are always warm with the juices of life and helpful for a modern reader. But there is also Saul Bellow and Heinrich Böll, Francois Mauriac and William Faulkner, W. H. Auden and Paul Claudel, Pablo Neruda and Nikos Kazantzakis, Jorge Luis Borges and Rainer Maria Rilke, and the dozens of others who deal with eternal verities in a rich and significant way. We are not expected to agree with them, but if either their content or their style provoke us into creativity, it was worth the trip to the library.

A young associate pastor complained after only six months in his first assignment, "I find it almost impossible to preach anymore; I feel dried up." Had he considered reading a book? For almost any important book is full of ideas, questions, and challenges. Any serious author, old or new, can become our partner in a dialogue which may result in anger, argument, or delight, but will almost certainly nudge us toward more imaginative preaching.

Interesting persons make interesting preachers. A person who is dull, uninvolved in life, with a mind as bland as custard, will not suddenly become exciting upon entering a pulpit. While it is true that many interesting people read quite widely, others have sharpened their curiosity about people and life through a wide range of experiences.

I have often been pleased to notice the way clinical pastoral education quarters give seminarians memorable experiences which invariably find their way into their sermons. I am sure C.P.E. has other good results, but there can be no doubt that encounters with the sick, the hospital staffs, chaplains of other faiths, and all of the people in the program produce more interesting students who then, drawing upon their recent experiences, produce more interesting sermons.

If possible, jobs and field education programs should be both varied and challenging during student years since these early impressions are lasting and will be much mined for stories and examples in the first years of ministry. The minister who has been in the Navy or the Peace Corps, or who has worked as a waiter or a salesman or an actor, or who has lived in a different city may not be any brighter than a classmate who has done none of these things, but at least he should have some interesting stories. Contact with people of different social and economic backgrounds, different races and religions, and different languages and world-views forces us to respond in unaccustomed ways. We must be (or at least we should be) creative in our reactions to break out of highly predictable routines.

My parents encouraged me, at the age of nineteen, to travel through Mexico. With little money and little Spanish, but with constant wonder, I discovered an ancient culture and a most *simpático* people. That was the beginning of a long interest in Latin America and a deepening appreciation of its heritage. Although, contrary to popular opinion, travel is not always broadening, it has often been a stimulus for the imagination. Although the thousands of young tourists who invade Europe every summer do not all have an equal curiosity and openness to the cultures they enter, some will find themselves asking new questions and searching for new answers.

I know, for example, what happened to my own imagination when, two years ago, I visited the Auschwitz concentration camp in southern Poland. Even though I had seen Dachau in West Germany and Buchenwald in East Germany, I was not prepared for this place, the largest of all the extermination camps and the best preserved. Rooms full of suitcases brought by the prisoners, hundreds and hundreds of shoes, cases full of hair, eyeglasses, children's clothes and toys, and the long rows of photographs of frightened men and women in their striped uniforms; the gate with its inscription of *Arbeit Macht Frei*, the watchtowers, the terrible ovens, and the wall where so many were shot. The Communist authorities do not encourage any memories of the many clergymen who died there, but I wanted to visit the cell of Father Maximilian Kolbe, a Polish Franciscan priest who had volunteered to take the place of another man condemned to die by starvation. An old woman near the gate told me in German that I would find the cell where he died in the basement of Disciplinary Barracks Number Eleven. I found the cell, and with a bare light bulb breaking the darkness, saw that fresh flowers had been pushed through the bars and covered the floor where this man of the gospel had died in agony that a brother might live. Kolbe's last and greatest sermon was not preached with words but with lonely pain in this dark prison. Though he surely had said many fine and beautiful things about the Christian life in the earlier days of his ministry, it is his final act of love that is remembered by the man he saved—who is still alive today—and by millions of other Poles.

I was forced to consider my own ministry; I was forced to think of my own life as a priest and preacher of the gospel. Topics such as sacrifice and suffering could not remain abstractions in such a place. The mystery of sin and evil was no longer a chapter in a theology book, for at Auschwitz the ground is covered with the ashes of innocent people. But here too there had also been love and compassion. Travel had brought me experience, a more shattering experience than I had foreseen or desired, and had led to reflection, new ideas, and new decisions.

The insightful little comment, supposedly made by Karl Barth, that he prepared his sermon with the Bible in one hand and the daily newspaper in the other has been repeated *ad nauseam* in almost every book on preaching. But the point of it is no less important. We must be people of our day. I know a man who has been very successful in relating with young people. He listens to their radio programs, sees many films, and subscribes to magazines directed to a young market. Some might argue that listening to the lyrics of rock songs and too much disco could push many preachers over the brink into a breakdown. But even if our own tastes run to Mozart and Bartok, it may be a truly pastoral action to start listening to a station with a top-forty format. It would at least be educational to hear the explicit lyrics of a song like "Nice Girls Don't, But I Do," knowing that thousands of Christian young people are listening to the same text.

Harry Schlitt, working with the highly energetic Miles O'Brien Riley at the Communications Center in San Francisco, probably preaches to more teens and young adults than anyone else in the Bay area. By carefully timing a message, often with a touch of humor and always with a dash of imagination, to bridge the top forty songs, he fashions a radio spot that is played again and again on the most popular stations. The messages are usually biblical, but done in an idiom that appeals to rock station managers and their listeners. Every week they change. The very words of the songs provide a springboard for a clever Christian comment. Yes, clever! Are the cynical comments of the agnostics to be the only clever ones?

For those who need a label, Harry's work may be called pre-evangelization; it would seem that pre-evangelization is just the kind of preaching that is called for in the tumultuous and permissive California scene. It is, after all, the care and love which a preacher has for the potential audience which allows imaginative leaps to be made. Our people may be flower children going to seed by the Golden Gate, seniors playing shuffleboard in St. Petersburg, farmers in Minnesota, undergraduates at a state university, or auto workers in Detroit—all of them are deaf to the highly predictable.

There is a law in communications theory which says that the more predictable a message is, the less information is transmitted. To say that two and two equals four does not really tell us much; it is so very predictable. We can also say that the more predictable a sermon is, the less interest is aroused. Our problem is that the basic elements of the gospel have become by this time highly predictable. Almost the whole of the western world feels that the Jesus story is "old hat." Never mind that vast numbers have heard only a sketchy outline of Christian teaching; never mind that millions are grossly misinformed. They think that they can predict not only the content but the very style and tone of voice. When President Carter gave his long-awaited energy talk, it was quickly damned with faint praise. It was called a "sermon," and everyone's heard enough of those!

Even the setting for our preaching holds few surprises. A highly predictable message is given by a predictable person dressed in a predictable way in a predictable place at a predictable time! To say that the gospel needs to be repeated in season and out of season is to miss the point if we cannot stimulate interest and maintain attention once we have it. Therefore we need a touch of the unpredictable, the element of surprise, something that will make the good news wonderful and new again. We ourselves would not have given our lives to the Christian cause if we had not found it to be dramatic, challenging, and powerful. We want to share the excitement which the early Christians felt and which we feel. We want men and women of our generation to hear the gospel with all the freshness and appeal that it had when it was first spoken in Galilee or Judea or repeated in some humble house church in Corinth or Rome. We cannot change its content; we cannot introduce some doctrinal novelty, but we can use our imaginations to break the stereotypes. We can, as it were, sharpen the blade of a two-edged sword with our God-given creativity.

OPENNESS TO CREATIVITY

Our customary thinking is usually judgmental, and it tends to be negative. What holes can I find in this argument? What is wrong with the idea being presented? Isn't this approach foolish and ill-advised? I foresee many difficulties that will surely occur. Let's be careful and prudent. However, as Alex Osborn remarks:

> Judgment and imagination can help each other if kept apart when they should be kept apart. In creative effort we have to be a Jekyll-and-Hyde. From time to time, we must turn off our judicial mind and light up our creative mind. And we must wait long enough before turning up our judicial light again. Otherwise, premature judgment may douse our creative flames, and even wash away ideas already generated. Especially in approaching a creative problem, we should give imagination priority over judgment and let it roam around our objective. [1]

Although creative people certainly know periods of dismay and frustration, they do tend to be enthusiastic, welcoming the inspirations that come, and avoiding a strongly negative attitude.

Even in times of creative dryness they continue to hope for the bright new ideas. They trust in their imaginative faculty the way an actor trusts his memory on the stage or a football player trusts his muscular agility on the field. They learn to endure the cold water that highly judgmental people throw on them and their work because they preserve an inner confidence in their vision. There are moments of self-doubt, of course, but no lasting discouragement to destroy their creative vitality.

Many produce valuable work without support from friends or relatives, but there is no doubt that encouragement is an elixir of life. There is a harsh clerical witticism that maims and kills. Clergy seem to find it especially hard to praise or thank creative colleagues, and we can only wonder at the generosity that would have served the Kingdom but was instead nipped in the bud by the green-eyed monster of envy.

Many among the clergy, through inclination or training, are given to perfectionism. They forget that we can only *try* to be perfect as the heavenly Father is perfect, and when their creative efforts as well as their lives are flawed, future creative efforts are seriously cramped. There must be the freedom to risk something new and even laughable for the sake of the Kingdom. If we are fascinated with our own perfection, we are unlikely to become fools for Christ's sake. Creativity, after all, is usually an adventure and must allow for the possibility of a mistake.

For the person who is puzzled, perplexed, and vexed with the world, creativity is blocked. It is necessary to wonder; to taste and savor and delight in people and things and events. To see Queen Anne's lace instead of a summer weed; to breathe in the freshness of creation on the windy shores of Lake Superior. And then to go further: to hear the wail of a baby in a Chicago housing project and know the sound of Bethlehem; to touch the crucified Christ in a nursing home; to stand in Easter awe as a man or woman dies to a lifetime of selfishness and sin and rises to new life. The gift of faith opens us to wonder, and wonder opens us to ourselves, to others, to the whole world. The mystery of existence is never neatly resolved, only more deeply appreciated.

FINDING NEW IDEAS

The production of new ideas is of great importance in the world of business. Millions of dollars are spent on research laboratories and finding "creative" people who will generate new or improved products, new names, packaging, promotional schemes, and so-called "inspired hypotheses." It has been discovered that you can deliberately increase production of good ideas by following two basic principles. The first is "deferment of judgment." Much harm is done in the creative process by moving in too quickly with a decision which will cut off other possible leads. We are anxious for a solution; we want to get the sermon finished quickly and move on to other business. For example, we read the Gospel text for the coming Sunday. An idea comes, and we gleefully grab it and develop it. We have our sermon, a rather miserable thing, to be sure, because we followed the first idea or two that came along. When we grab something off the top of our heads, it is usually shallow and trite. How often is a sermon preached by an adult preacher which completely ignores recent biblical scholarship and mature theology and instead presents an approach to a passage which was learned as a child in Sunday school. It happened to be the first thing remembered when the passage was read. We have not lived with the text, but rather have opted for a quick judgment, putting an end to alternative ideas. Other possibilities are unfortunately rejected in favor of the initial inferior idea.

The second principle is that "quantity breeds quality." The more ideas that are produced, the more likely it is that we will think up some that are truly good. It is generally understood that the best ideas seldom come first. One study showed that during a sustained effort to produce ideas, the second half of the time provided 78 percent more good ideas than the first half of the period. Beethoven constantly revised and improved his scores; it is interesting to compare his rather banal first efforts with the originality and power of the final piece.

The preacher also needs many ideas, a richness of materials. How sad it is that so many preachers, both Protestant and Catholic, subscribe to expensive homiletic services which provide not an abundance of stimuli for creativity but rather a precooked idea or two to be reheated for the hapless congregation. These "aids" (or in some cases completely canned sermons) are often pounded out by some unknown writer (doing the Christmas sermons in July!) who knows neither the people nor the place where they will be used. It is not just that the all-purpose sermon is a bad sermon and that the people have been given a tasteless and inadequate diet. The preacher has also been deprived. He or she has avoided the struggle to see and so there has been no insight, no effort, and no joy.

A friend of mine is a good amateur chef. His specialty is Italian cuisine which depends on very fresh ingredients, spices, and wine. He goes first to a market where there is a rich variety of possible foods for the meal which he is planning. After looking at the many things which are available, he selects, perhaps, some fish which looks especially fresh that day. Of course when he makes sauce for the pasta, fish, or veal it will be carefully prepared with the right seasonings and left to simmer for a long time. When the pasta is *al dente* and everything is just right, he dramatically pours the sauce and serves the meal with style. It will both taste and look magnificent.

The creative production of a sermon is analogous. First the preacher will become aware of a rich variety of ideas. He will not clutch the first thing he notices, but feast his senses on the distinctiveness of each idea. At last he will choose several interesting ideas, including a central one which seems especially fresh and important for the particular group. But still he will not rush to make everything final. There must be the long simmering, if possible over several days, for the flavor of the ideas to be brought out, for some ingredients to melt and blend. Ultimately the time comes for the final preparation and presentation. Things should be served piping hot and with *élan*. The feast of words should both nourish and stimulate.

Walter J. Burghardt has described his sermon preparation. First there are the hours spent in research, in gathering sheer information about the text; then there's the time spent mulling over what the scriptural data might have to say to a certain community today, until a promising central idea bursts forth.

"From that point my hours are given over to . . . words. Precisely here is a preacher's crucifixion. A word is not an entry in Webster; it is colored by living experience. The Eucharist is indeed a bread that gives life; but when *you* hear the word of "life," you hear something quite different from the 200,000 skin-and-bones starving who "live" in the streets of Calcutta, build tiny fires to cook scraps of food, defecate at curbstones, curl up against a wall to sleep—perhaps to die. Yes, a word is real, is sacred, is powerful, but inevitably a word is . . . I. This makes a double demand on a preacher: I must sense what my people hear, and I must say what I mean. [2]

But of course, it is not merely clarity that is sought. A word is to be a challenge, a summons to decision, moving the listeners to fashion their lives in accordance with what is said. Burghardt continues:

If I am to persuade, my whole person should be aflame with what I proclaim. If I am to move, the words I utter must be chosen with care and love, with sweat and fire. That is why, before I set pen to paper, I listen to Beethoven or Tchaikovsky, Vivaldi or Mary Lou Williams, Edith Piaf or the theme from "Doctor Zhivago"; I read poetry aloud, Shakespeare or Hopkins, T. S. Eliot or e.e. cummings—something to turn me on, so that the end result will not sound like a Roman rescript or a laundry list. To challenge, the word must come alive. [3]

Some would claim that in the creative process (and the preparation of a sermon should be such) there comes a peak moment of illumination. The light bulb goes on suddenly in the mind and in the heart. We burst out with "Aha! Eureka! I've got it!"

Most people involved in creative work would say that this is sometimes the case. But only sometimes. The sudden flashes of light are wonderful if and when they come. But for most productive people, especially those who must face automatic deadlines, it is a question of getting started, gathering appropriate materials, and, with a good deal of effort, mixing them into something "original." How many musicians have taken melodies from the folk tunes of their countries or from a band playing in the streets of Vienna or Budapest? Shakespeare took some of his plots from Roman comedies and Italian tales. The important thing is what they did with the raw materials. New relationships are discovered among various elements. There are mutations and alterations. The original tune is changed from major to minor and played on bagpipes! The setting of the story is moved from the time of Boccaccio to the twentieth century. Picasso takes a classical composition and paints it in an abstract manner. And the creative preacher finds that something similar must be done on a regular basis.

As Osborn remarks:

> A minister's weekly deadline badgers him into creative action. At Sunday dinner we are likely to say "Wasn't that a wonderful sermon this morning?" We seldom stop to think how tremendous was the creative effort that went into that message. The basic idea of each sermon—just that alone—requires more creative juice each week than most of us generate in a month. And, beyond the theme, some 50 other ideas have to be thought up to give power and sparkle to each sermon.[4]

But let us also admit that we do not labor in some mean quarry digging out cold stones to use as the building blocks of our sermons. Rather, to find our theme and a few of the "50 other ideas" we open a true treasure chest containing a richness beyond compare. Beethoven may have heard a fragment of a military march outside his window and transformed it into a symphonic movement; Chaucer did wonders with some popular racy tales; Shakespeare used his magic on some Roman farces and medieval legends. But the preacher goes with weekly wonder into a collection of human experience and poetry of the highest quality. The Bible, even if seen only from the point of view of the secular literary critic, is obviously an anthology of masterpieces.

Like a magnificent Steinway grand piano, well tuned and with open strings, just a touch anywhere will start the overtones; a chord played *forte* will start reverberations throughout the concert hall and in the hearts of the audience. So, too, as we approach the Bible with wonder and expectancy we find that its strings are alive and waiting to be played. Because it is a record of human experience, men and women in relationship with each other and with God, its keyboard is large and varied, from deep and majestic notes in the bass to the brightest of treble sounds. If our interpretation has even a modicum of skill and feeling, the miracle of empathy takes place. There is a sharing of meaning and emotion.

The Bible, like the concert grand, is a splendid work of art in itself, but it needs someone to play it, to allow it to sing. It began as the oral expression of what real people experienced, and it is to continue as such. The Scriptures ask for a loving interpretation by a preacher who cares.

THE PREACHER AS ARTIST

We preachers have been reluctant to think of ourselves as poets and artists. As theologians, yes. As exegetes, psychologists, counselors, communicators, persuaders, rhetoricians, pastors, yes! But to be an artist, a poet, sounds too extraordinary, demanding special gifts far beyond us. And yet the sermon, like art itself, must be "the revealing experience." Karl Rahner puts it this way:

> To the poet is entrusted the word. He is a man who can utter the great words pregnantly *(verdichtet)*. Every man speaks great words—as long as he has not sunk into a spiritual death. Everyone calls things by their names and in so doing, continues the work of Adam his father. But the poet has the vocation and the gift of saying such words pregnantly. He may say them in such a way that through his words, the things—as though set free—enter into the light of others who hear the word of the poet. . . . He [God] can come in no way other than as the word—without taking us already away from the world to Himself. For He should give Himself to us precisely in that which He simply as the Creator of realities outside Himself cannot reveal. This is possible only because there is something—one thing only—in the world which belongs to God's own reality: that reference redeemed from muteness, that reference which points beyond all created things—the word.[5]

We have been entrusted with the word. We become artists with language. Luis Alonso Schökel has given a sketch of an artist in our own culture. Do we find in it our own likeness?

> Usually, he is a man possessing a capacity to experience many things intensely. These experiences need not be specifically poetic; much of what he lives is shared by the lot of men. . . . He is capable of deeply

personal experiences and at the same time, by reason of some
mysterious sympathy with men and things, he can enter into the
experience of others and relive them. Life itself breaks in to make its
impact and set up these intense vibrations, but then, so does
literature. . . . In art, a man gives himself up to his experiences,
admitting all their vividness and their pain. . . . However, a man
must be somewhat detached from an experience, be it his own or
another's if he is to write of it. A great artist begins with an intuition
which forms the dominant life center and unifying principle of his
work. . . . Finally, the literary artist has the gift of language.[6]

The process is in four steps: experience, reflective vision,
intuition, and execution. Life must break in on us and make its
impact (perhaps this explains why student preachers have great
difficulty in giving a funeral homily: life has not yet brought them the
experience of the death of a loved one; indeed, their grandparents
may still be living). But, as Schökel says, literature also breaks in
upon the artist.

There is reason to doubt that one can ever be the preacher-artist if
biblical literature has never "broken in" on one's consciousness,
probably fairly early in life. André Malraux states in *The Voices of
Silence:*

One of the reasons why the artist's way of seeing differs so greatly from
that of the ordinary man is that it has been conditioned, from the
start, by the paintings and statues he has seen; by the world of art. It is
a revealing fact that, when explaining how his vocation came to him,
every great artist traces it back to the emotion he experienced at his
contact with some specific work of art: a writer to the reading of a
poem or novel (or perhaps a visit to the theater); a musician to a
concert he attended; a painter to a painting he once saw. Never do we
hear of a man who, out of the blue so to speak, feels a compulsion to
"express" some scene or startling incident.[7]

So too, the preacher must be "conditioned" by the biblical
literature; it must, usually over a period of time, be allowed to do its
work, to challenge, to excite, to provoke, to generate enthusiasm, to
imprint itself deeply on the preacher's soul. For the preacher must in
some way identify himself or herself with the text if it is to be
experienced. The mystery of empathy must take place in the speaker

before it can take place in the listeners. There must be identification between the scriptural text, the preacher, and finally the congregation. The feelings expressed by the poet who wrote the text are felt by the preacher both before and during the sermon and—if the sermon is a success—are felt by the congregation in the pews. Rollo May says of empathy:

> Thus people speak of music "carrying them away," or of the violin playing upon the strings of their emotions, or of the changing colors of the sunset creating a corresponding change in their emotions. Jung makes empathy the center of his theory of aesthetics. The person looking at the artistic object, he says, "becomes the object; he identifies himself with it, and in this way gets rid of himself."[8]

Without this ability to act and feel as if we were someone else, we do not get to the inside of the poem. We can remain a critic or a student of the poem, but we do not participate in it and, in a real sense, we do not understand it. (And the Bible, of course, must be seen as a series of poems.) This may help explain why some great biblical scholars and theologians can spend a lifetime reading the Gospels and remain agnostics. For unlike secular drama where "there occurs the very obvious identification of the actors with the fictitious characters they are representing, as well as the more subtle identification of the observers with the actors,"[9] Jesus and the people who surround him are not fictitious.

I approach the "poem" which is St. Luke's or St. John's Gospel. There is surely no excess of details, or "purple patches" of description. Yet, with great economy, cues are given to shape character. In lieu of stage directions, I respond to those cues and build an interpretation of the characters and narrator (for the biblical narrators are definitely not the disinterested third-person voices of some modern novels, but are much involved and possess distinctive points of view.) Unlike many plays where I may identify with only one character, the Gospels and much of the Old Testament provide such an evocative presentation of people and their experiences that I find myself identifying with many characters. Like other pieces of great literature, certain biblical texts have the power of calling forth the many persons that are in each of us. For in everyone there is not

only the man, but also the woman; not only the old person, but also
the little child; not only the saint, but also the sinner. I identify with
the prodigal son—but also with the father, the elder brother, and
perhaps even the servant. I identify with Jesus and with Peter, with
Magdalene and with Judas, with Mary and with Joseph. I feel their
feelings and think their thoughts. Although I may speak with a bass
voice, my interpretation of the Magnificat, for example, follows the
mind and heart of Mary. I give myself over to the text; I surrender to
the thoughts and feelings which are there.

However, for most of us this is not necessarily an easy surrender.
The Bible contains more than piety and gentleness. If we are not
Semitic or at least Mediterranean, the violent emotions which leap
out at us from so many of the pages frighten and intimidate. There is
searing sarcasm and hatred, fury and violence. Babies have their
brains smashed against a wall; children are murdered by despotic
kings; there are bloody wars and painful executions. The Bible is the
story of Semites who feel deeply and intensely, not of sophisticated
Parisians or cool Bostonians.

A year or so ago a couple of Palestinian Liberation Organization
men infiltrated northern Israel and killed some Jewish children in a
school. One of the terrorists managed to hold out for a time on the
upper floor of a building. The television cameras quickly got to the
scene and recorded some footage for the afternoon news. The
mother of one of the murdered children was in front of the building
where the terrorist was still hiding. The camera came in for a close
shot of her face. We suddenly saw a modern Rachel weeping for her
child. But more than weeping. She screamed, and she cursed.
People pulled on her arms to hold her back. Her grief was not
restrained and decorous. Her sobs were not genteel but full of fury.
She wanted to rush into that building, catch the murderer of her
child, and pull him apart, limb from limb. The scene could have
been lifted directly from the pages of the Old Testament.

The colors of the Bible are not shades of discreet gray or muted
beige; they are primary colors for the most part, livid and strong.
People experience much passion, the intense feelings of love and
envy, naked ambition and wild delight, abject sorrow and burning
remorse. King David dances and leaps in the street. A woman washes

the Lord's feet with her tears; Peter quickly cuts off the servant's ear. In general, they are not a very subtle and nuanced crowd. Even the words of Jesus—"brood of vipers, whitened sepulchres!"—indicate a powerful anger. It takes a strong emotion indeed to motivate someone to use that kind of language.

It is not right to drain the Bible of the emotions that are there. We are not to add, but neither are we to subtract. As interpreters who care about the text, we must come to it ready to learn and to experience what is already there. Then we can respond in a creative way. This means, of course, a close reading of the text. We do not ordinarily get beneath the surface of any literature with a superficial reading. The Bible is a special challenge because it is so ancient and because it includes so many styles and authors. Are we reading the words of an ancient liturgical hymn? How does this letter differ from our modern letters? What are the poetic devices used in this psalm? Questions should rise out of the text as we go into it more deeply. What gesture accompanied this phrase when it was spoken? What motivated this harsh or gentle response? To whom was this line spoken? There are important questions of mood and atmosphere. Some answers may come from a study of the scholarly commentaries but other answers appear as we become more and more familiar with the text itself.

A good example of a young preacher who allows the text the opportunity to work on him and mold his preaching is Marc Pasciak. While he was still in the seminary he began to memorize the Sunday Gospel reading each week. When he was assigned as an associate pastor at a large Chicago parish, he continued to do the same. I asked him to describe his method.

> On Monday I read through the Gospel passage for the following Sunday several times. On Tuesday I read it several times again, aloud and still more carefully. On Wednesday and Thursday I continue reading it and have it almost memorized. By this time the homily begins to take shape. On Friday and Saturday I polish the homily and complete my interpretation of the gospel. On Sunday I do an oral interpretation of the gospel followed by a homily which is based on it.

For a week he has been living with a Gospel lesson, letting it sink into his mind and imagination as he works to memorize it. The images become familiar and more important, the characters fully realized, the emotions understood and experienced. The gospel itself is allowed to nourish the imagination. The homily almost seems "to be writing itself."

"And, you know," Marc added, "once you go through the three year cycle, it is easy to recall them the second time around. Also, I don't have to carry a Bible when I visit the sick in their homes or the hospitals; I can just tell them the gospel that they seem to need."

"What do the people in your parish think?"

"At first they were surprised that I had memorized the whole gospel. But they certainly pay attention better when there is a full interpretation. They like it!"

When we as preachers prepare our scriptural readings with such care, trying to present the full intellectual and emotional content, a true oral interpretation of everything we can discover in the text, we will find that the Bible itself is the greatest stimulus for creative preaching. In doing this, we are part of a long and noble tradition. Lucien Deiss, in speaking of the homily in the synagogue service, observes:

> The preacher took the sacred text outside its temporal and historical context, and pored over it endlessly, examining it with all his intellectual resources and with a stubbornness born of love. In order to nourish faith and influence life, he tried to make the word even more desirable and delightful. "If man explains the words of the Torah in public and does not make them more tasteful than milk and honey," says one midrash "it would be better for him to say nothing." It was also said that it should be as much a delight to listen to the words of the law as to gaze upon a newly married girl as she sits beneath the nuptial canopy. Thus the reading service was considered a feast. For this reason no one was to begin or end the readings with a text of ill omen. [10]

Early Christian authors also ask for this slow and involved reading of the sacred text. The reader is to "taste" and "savor" the words, "chewing them like a cow chews its cud." If this image lacks charm, it at least makes its point! We are to feed ourselves on the words of sacred Scripture, getting all the juices and nourishment out of them that we can.

Taking this kind of time and care with the text, reading it aloud, responding emotionally not only with the voice but with a deep involvement of the senses, both a kinetic and kinesthetic response, will be a fascinating experience for the reader. Most of us were trained to be "speed readers," content to skim off a few ideas or a bit of data. We have often looked upon the Bible as the great theological cupboard full of proof texts instead of inspired literature full of life. Even our muscle tone must change as we respond to the text; we must get shivers down our spine as we listen to Jesus speak by the lake; our hands should get clammy as we follow him through the passion to Calvary; our very posture should change when we read of the Easter events. From this encounter with Jesus, this deep experience of what happened, can come insight. We may, God willing, receive the intuition which provides the directive energy and force for making the word of Scripture a word for today. If we feel the tingle of excitement down our backbone as we interpret orally the words of Christ, there is at least a chance that the people will feel it too. And this sharing of wonder and beauty may lead to many good things.

After primary creativeness, the imaginative spark, must come secondary creativeness, which we can translate as hard work! As A. H. Maslow says:

> I am very certain that many, many people have waked up in the middle of the night with a flash of inspiration about some novel they would like to write, or a play or a poem or whatever and that most of these inspirations never came to anything. Inspirations are a dime a dozen. The difference between the inspiration and the final product, for example, Tolstoy's *War and Peace*, is an awful lot of hard work, an awful lot of discipline, an awful lot of training, an awful lot of finger exercises and practices and rehearsals and throwing away first drafts and so on. Now the virtues which go with the secondary kind of creativeness, the creativeness which results in the actual products, in the great paintings, the great novels, in the bridges, the new inventions, and so on, rest as heavily upon other virtues—stubborness and patience and hard work and so on—as they do upon the creativeness of the personality.[11]

Especially for any extended work, a symphony, a novel, or a series of sermons, there can be no doubt that Maslow is right. To face the sheets of flat white paper and the typewriter does demand a certain stubbornness and industry. But what motivates the hard work and the burning of the midnight oil? Some very productive artists worked to make money. Bach and Mozart produced some beautiful music in order to pay their bills. Others thought of fame, making something that would be a kind of monument, giving a measure of immortality. Others have felt that their art gave meaning to their lives; art helped them to know that they were alive and had some purpose. Still others liked to entertain and produced for the sheer pleasure it would give other people. And some, especially in an earlier age, saw their creativity as an act of religion. They made something for the honor and glory of God.

Stephen Spender, the English poet, speaks of a "spiritual compulsion." Some speak of visions and special missions. Picasso said, "The essential in these times of moral misery is to create enthusiasm." Others are driven people; Emily Dickinson needed to write poems, which she then hid in a desk drawer. As Picasso proclaimed, "The artist is a receptacle of emotions come from no matter where; from the sky, the earth, a piece of paper, a passing figure, a cobweb."

But what of us, the Christian preachers? Could our motivation contain elements of any or all of these varied intentions? It is not impossible; and yet none of them suffice. It is not even enough to consider the composition of our sermon in the same way that a medieval craftsman thought of his work in stone or stained glass. Georges Rouault, perhaps the greatest religious painter of this century, once said that he wanted to paint the face of Christ that would break the heart of the world. The pious Bach, the devout Rouault, the unknown master of the Pietà of Avignon, and the painter of the icon of Our Lady of Vladimir—all, we may presume, worked for the Lord, for his honor and his glory. Their labor became an act of adoration, and their art was often bathed in a religious intensity which we can feel today.

But the preacher goes further, beyond even so lofty an inspiration. The preacher not only works *for* Christ; the preacher works *with* him. A theologian may speak words about God, but the preacher speaks God's word. If theology is "faith seeking understanding," then preaching is "faith finding expression." No one cooperates more closely with God in his creative and revealing work, no one is more "present" and more engaged in the coming of the Kingdom, no human being is more important in the generation of faith than the person who announces the gospel. We must have, therefore, a loving attentiveness to the spirit within us—and that, of course, is spirituality. As Burghardt says:

> Ultimately, I am the word, the word that is heard. And—I say it fearfully—it is not a clever rhetorician the people need, but a holy homilist. Holy in what sense? Because aware that I am only *a* word, not *the* word: if God does not speak through me, I am "a noisy gong, a clanging cymbal" (1 Cor. 13:1). Because my homily is a prayer: in preparation and pulpit, I stand before God in praise of him, not of my own rhetorical perfection. Because aware of my own weakness: I too need the word I preach, I too need forgiveness, I too am vulnerable, I am a *wounded* healer. Because, like my hearers, I too ceaselessly murmur: "I believe, Lord; help my unbelief." Because I am in love: with the things of God, with the people of God, with God himself. Because the hungers of God's family are my hungers: when they bleed, I weep. Unless some of this breaks through, the word may indeed be proclaimed, but it will hardly be heard. The word is . . . I.[12]

V. "CHRIST PREACHES CHRIST"

In the middle of the "pool of nectar" at Amritsar in the Punjab stands the golden temple of the Sikhs. Here appointed men sit and read from the holy book in half-hour shifts until, every forty-eight hours, a reading is completed and the pages are turned back to the beginning. The reading never stops; the words are constantly proclaimed and the wisdom transmitted.

Many religious leaders and founders of philosophies and theologies that have attracted a following have died and left a legacy, often written, to be transmitted after their death. Their followers have faithfully guarded it and proclaimed it. Mormons and Moslems, Buddists and Hindus, Christian Scientists and Sikhs, all strive to preserve their religious heritage and pass it on to a new generation. Marxists and other philosophers seem to be less successful, though they are equally loyal and energetic.

If we Christian preachers follow a juridical theology of redemption, in which Christ once acquired the merits of our salvation and then allowed them to be applied later, we may be content to be transmitters of what is recorded in Scripture, going forth with a good memory and a holy book to preserve the words of our founder. But Christ, unlike Mohammed, Joseph Smith, and Mary Baker Eddy, has not withdrawn from this world and from his church. Rather, he has become our salvation (1 Cor. 1:30). He is the living vine of which we must be the branches. He is present, for now he has come to us as he promised (John 14:18).

"By raising Christ, God effects salvation in him and at the same time offers to men this Christ who has become their salvation. The resurrection is incarnation in fullness: both total sanctification of Christ in God and total sending into the world (John 10:36; 17:18-19)."[1]

Christ is the Gospel; he is salvation; he is the object of faith. To have faith is to possess Jesus Christ. Therefore Christian preaching is not an exercise in teaching a body of truths, in passing on sacred texts, or even in attesting to important facts. It must give Jesus Christ; it must convey his presence. Far more than an intellectual assent, Christian faith is a commitment of life, of one's future, a total redirecting of energy and thought and action. Surely this will happen only when there is an encounter with Christ. The one who would come to faith must see Jesus Christ who is the revelatory sign of his mystery (cf. John 1:14). He himself opens our eyes so that we may see his glory and share in his mystery. He comes in person. Christ coming is Christian preaching.

> God evangelizes the world by raising Jesus Christ, the good news is proclaimed by the divine action glorifying Christ. In his resurrection, Christ is preached and believed by men and he it is—in his resurrection—who is God's preaching to men, the cause of faith. The object of faith is also its source. Christian preaching therefore has deep roots: in the mystery of God, begetting Jesus Christ through the Holy Spirit (Rom. 8:11) for men.[2]

It follows that preaching is not merely to muster solid arguments which will lead to faith (the most cogent being the resurrection), but rather to show Christ, whose resurrection is final salvation coming into the world.

> Preaching is not as much an apologia for Christ as his epiphany; it results from the action of divine power which raises Christ for men. In this world, God raises Christ in the form of the kerygma, in the form of evangelization. By a unique action, God himself raises him to the fullness of salvation, offers him to men by preaching, draws them into fellowship with him, justifies them in him in faith.[3]

The Father utters the Word—who is Jesus. Jesus Christ not only preaches good news to the poor; he *is* that good news. And, in his wisdom, he invited apostles to be his representatives in order to bring about his presence for those in other places and other times. They are sent out to preach, bearing in their bodies the death of Jesus so that the life of Jesus might be revealed in their mortal flesh (2 Cor. 4:10-11). Down through the centuries each new generation must discover that Christ is truly present and—through human language—learn that a fully human encounter with him is possible. Words are used not merely for communication but to effect a communion.

> Words have this virtue, that through them a person expresses himself and goes out of himself, he is brought towards other men and himself acts in them with the aid of words. It is essential therefore for the Christian to remain in Christ and for Christ to remain in him (John 15:5) and then the miracle is achieved: this man's word becomes Christ's word, the radiance of Christ's dynamic presence. There is no Christian preaching without identification with Christ. If he does not remain in Christ, a Christian is lying about God, even if much of what he says is true: for he is not expressing the Truth, he is counterfeiting what the Father reveals to the world in begetting his Christ.[4]

Dare we think of ourselves as apostles? Only if we have seen Jesus our Lord (see 1 Cor. 9:1). Only if we can say with John, "We have seen and testify that the Father has sent his son as the Savior of the world" (1 John 4:14). It was given to only a few to be in Nazareth or Jerusalem or along the lake when Jesus walked there. But that, of course, is not the essential point. It is with the eyes of faith that all of us, Peter, Paul, John, or the modern preacher, see Christ as the Lord and Savior of the world. There must be an experience, but it will be a faith experience. There is the possibility—indeed the necessity—of being able to say with Christ that "we speak of what we know and bear witness to what we have seen" (John 3:11). Our testimony flows from a personal encounter with Christ.

The preacher who is present to Christ and to whom Christ is present is already in the process of a deep transformation. Christ takes possession of the preacher and profound changes take place. The preacher takes possession of the values and attitudes of Christ.

The apostle becomes the transparency of Christ. To the extent that the preacher is in union with Christ, the words of Christ are spoken, or—in the phrase of Augustine—"Christ preaches Christ."

The encounter with Christ through preaching becomes easier insofar as the apostle conforms mind and heart with the mind and heart of Christ. The pastor must radiate before the flock the lovable and kind features of Jesus Christ. The preacher must remain faithful to the mystery of Christian love so that the beauty and goodness of Christ may appear in words and actions. Although every Christian is called to holiness, how can we deny that those of us who preach must hear the call with special clarity?

PREACHING IS THE MEANS OF HOLINESS

Always there will be a certain interior tension. The apostles felt it and pastors feel it today. We are brothers and sisters among brothers and sisters. And yet we are also role models, teachers, shepherds following in the footsteps of the Good Shepherd. The Bishop of Rome may use the ancient title of "servant of the servants of God," but his authority is very great—as is the authority of anyone chosen by the church to proclaim God's word for today. We live among the people; we too must pay our bills and go to the dentist—but there is a difference. We are the "reverend" ones, the leaders of the Christian community and the examples of Christian living.

For many pastors (and sometimes their families), that has proved to be too great a strain. Not all are meant to be "public persons." Even Augustine expressed the paradox when he told his congregation: "For you I am a bishop, but with you I am a Christian." How often we want to say to our people: "For you I am your pastor, but with you I am also a poor sinner." Most congregations, of course, have long since taken their clergy down from their pedestals; a demythologizing of priests and ministers was long overdue. They appreciate our humanity much more and are usually quite prepared to forgive any number of foibles and idiosyncrasies. The veil of mystery that surrounded us has been pulled away, and we are found to be something less than demigods, neither all-wise nor all-good.

But while the pastor receives understanding for his drinking problem or inept administration (within certain limits!) and while a lack of social skills or good taste is discreetly overlooked, the pastor is expected to be, fundamentally, a person of the Kingdom. His or her fundamental option must be for the way of the gospel; there must be an obvious attempt to follow the way of Jesus and, in spite of occasional weaknesses and failings, to maintain a sincere friendship with him.

Many congregations have had to become quite blasé. They are not easily scandalized and admit to few surprises. But, from the most innocent to the most sophisticated, from the young to the old, the Christian people never seem to give up the expectation that their pastors be serious about sanctity. They are at least deeply saddened by the sinfulness and selfishness of the clergy. Many of them pray daily that we be holy.

But holiness, both the word and the reality, seems so full of ambiguities. The preacher, who must work closely and constantly with the gospel, sooner or later realizes that it will be understood only if we open our hearts to it completely. It is obviously not enough to read it and preach it. Tormented unbelievers have done as much in the history of the church. We must be converted by it, for those are holy who hear God's word and keep it.

And yet . . . our ministry is a busy one. So many sermons to prepare and deliver. Sick calls to make. Pastoral visitation in the homes. Funerals and wakes. Letters to write, and bills to pay. Counseling the troubled and confused. Youth groups and adult education programs. Weddings and baptisms. A funeral can wipe out a morning; telephone calls can eat away an afternoon; meetings in the evening followed by a little late television to relax—and another day bites the dust!

We would probably not be in the ministry if we had not had some initial conversion and the beginning of a friendship with Christ, but we honestly wonder if we are making any progress as Christians. In the midst of the important and the trivial activities which consume us each day, we doubt that we still pay loving attention to the words of our Friend and heed His suggestions. Are we closer to the mind and heart of Jesus now than we were ten years ago? Are we becoming ecclesiastical bureaucrats, not terribly evil, not terribly good, just very bland and very empty?

As seminarians we hated the very idea of lukewarm pastors; we had heard clearly what the Lord said about the lukewarm, and we agreed completely. But now, in a surprisingly short time, the novelty of pastoral life is over and we feel a dryness of spirit mixed with guilt. We are the ones who could be spit out! For some, the mockery of shattered ideals is too great and they may move close to despair. For others, the apostolate becomes tasteless and barren, the Bible a book of fables, all preaching hollow and deceptive, and religion reduced to nostalgia. To save their sanity they seek a job in the "real" world. It has, unhappily, been the history of thousands.

Union with Christ seemed somehow to be in competition with service to men and women. And serving men and women seemed clearly to be more urgent. Intimacy with God began to look like a spiritual luxury which the pressing demands of our people would not allow. Ministry wrestled with spirituality and the conflict could tear us apart. Something had to give. Usually, though not always, attentiveness to the spirit within us was postponed for some future time of psychic leisure.

In fact, however, the battle was not necessary! We did not have to choose between being a monk or a social worker. Our ministry is not in competition with holiness. We are sent forth as the first apostles were to work out our own salvation in the fulfillment of our mission. Our preaching mission is itself the way we deepen our union with Jesus. Preaching is the means to holiness.

Isn't it an idle question to ask whether preaching or prayer has primacy? Preaching, at its best, becomes prayer. And prayer gives the pastor the life and motivation to preach. It is folly to think that one can fulfill the function of preaching and not fully live the mystery we announce. We are incomplete as apostles without either prayer or preaching; our happiness and our success are bound up with both of these activities.

Preaching is not peripheral to our identity. Luther went so far as to state that the priest who does not preach ceases to be a priest. However, although Protestantism has officially always had a great respect for the pulpit, many ministers in recent years have questioned its value and preferred other kinds of pastoral service. Until the Second Vatican Council, I am sure that many priests in the Catholic Church would not have placed preaching among their top pastoral priorities. Now, however, the official teaching is most clear: "The People of God find unity first of all through the Word of the living God, which is quite properly sought from the lips of priests. Since no one can be saved who has not first believed, priests, as co-workers with their bishops, have as their primary duty the proclamation of the Gospel of God to all" (Decree on the Ministry and Life of Priests, No. 4).

Neither Protestant nor Catholic clergy would claim that the proclamation of the Gospel is a private clerical responsibility. It is the duty of the whole people of God. Nevertheless, it is now obligatory for Catholic priests and, I suspect, equally urgent for Protestant ministers to see it as their primary function. Miglarese describes this primary quality of the ministry of the Word as "foundational," that is: "(a) preliminary to and leading into further ministerial activity and responsibility; (b) supporting and sustaining all ministry that follows."[5]

It is impossible, therefore, to have a spirituality for ministers of the Word which neglects or merely tolerates their primary function. For is not the Gospel "foundational" in still another sense, that is, being the instrumental cause of a ever-deepening friendship with the Lord? All of us as Christians must go on responding to the continual calls God makes on us, whether they come from within or manifest themselves through people around us or in the events of our lives. Surely the demands of our primary responsibility indicate God's will for us and, as Dante said, "in his will is our peace." Our preaching apostolate is the way we do God's will. And doing his will leads to holiness, and to the peace and happiness which flow from it.

The conflict between our ministry and spirituality may have come about in trying to impose a rigorous schedule on something so fluid and dynamic as life. Schedules used to satisfy the rather recent need for organized productivity and neatness, but they also left a feeling of being fragmented and harassed by the hands of the clock. For the preacher, as for almost everyone else, the ideal was a time or "slot" for everything. There was to be a certain time for work, a time for eating, a time for light reading, a time for physical exercise, and—among many other items—a time for prayer. The well-organized preacher had only to make up a good horarium, fill in the appointment book, and there should be "a place for everything and everything in its place." But there are few people, especially those who must be creative and also attentively caring for the needs of others, who can operate like a well-oiled machine. Soon certain inexorable deadlines plus the sudden demands of telephone, doorbell, and daily correspondence had rubbed out the "slots" of less insistent activities: the arts, serious reading, recreation, and prayer.

It is time to integrate. Many preachers have arrived at the point where they realize that reading the news, biographies, and even a good novel is not wasted time, but rather remote preparation for the production of a homily. Are we able to go a step further and see prayer and sermon preparation as one?

Someone once asked Bishop Sheen how long it took him to prepare his latest sermon. "Forty-five years," he answered. And I don't think he meant to be cute! Forty-five years of meeting people, reading, teaching philosophy in the university, spending a daily hour in private prayer, celebrating the Eucharist—in a word, forty-five years of living open to the spirit and its promptings. The proximate preparation may have taken a few hours, but the remote preparation was a matter of years.

But is there a way by which even the proximate preparation is, in itself, a prayer? Must, at least, the final hours be kept separate from prayer, or may they also become integrated into our spiritual life? I would like to suggest contemplation as the integrating experience for the preacher.

THE CONTEMPLATIVE EXPERIENCE

It is necessary, I think, to state immediately that contemplation is practiced by many people who are not monks or cloistered nuns. It is surely not meant only for those who live in quiet places and with the time for long hours in church. It is, quite simply, a form of imaginative presence to the mysteries of the gospel. By "mystery" is meant any story unit of the Bible in which God is acting in human history. Ignatius of Loyola (who, together with Luther, could probably share the title of "most important religious figure of the sixteenth century") popularized, but did not invent, this form of prayer. He directed those making his "Spiritual Exercises" to enter into the mysteries by using all of the senses and faculties, "seeing the persons," "hearing what they are saying," and "considering what they are doing."

The biblical story thus becomes a current event, God's action which is going on at this very moment since I am there through the gift of my imagination. The particular scene becomes real for me, actualized at that moment in its eternal significance. I walk into the action; I become a member of the crowd listening to Jesus by the lake or one of the disciples in the boat. I may feel that I am there or that I identify with one of the historical persons involved in the mystery.

I am in the stable at Bethlehem; I feel the cold of the nightwind; I smell the straw and the animals; I pick up the child and hold him in my arms, experiencing his weight and hearing his wail; I begin to express my feelings to Mary and Joseph; I am starting to understand and to pray.

> It should be emphasized that the mysteries in question are not to be merely reconstructed by an imaginary return to the past, and entered into by a sort of movie-making effort of the fantasy. This is not, in fact, how people who contemplate them actually experience the mysteries. Because Christ is risen, all his mysteries somehow partake in his eternal now, and become really present to the person at prayer. However difficult it may be to explain this fact logically, the fact itself has long been recognized in the annual feasts of the liturgy. Christmas is much more than the remembering of an ancient birth: it is that birth itself made real among us now; and at Easter we say not merely that Jesus arose from the dead long ago, but that he is risen today in our midst. In the same way, closely related as they are to the central paschal mystery itself, all the other mysteries of scripture are realized in the now of prayer."[6]

We experience the sacred events as actually happening to us.

The principal object of prayer is, of course, not the production of next Sunday's sermon. It is the following of Christ. By entering into the events of Jesus' earthly life, by being present as Jesus calms the sea, cures the blind man, enters Jerusalem, carries his cross, or appears in the midst of the disciples in the upper room, we begin to see the contemporary plan for the salvation of our world and how we fit into it here and now. When we are there with Jesus during his agony in the garden or on Calvary, we are not involved in a costume drama, an edifying tableau for a Good Friday service. We are there in order to become more aware of our own involvement in the contemporary living out of the passion of the Lord. Just how do we make up what is lacking in the sufferings of Jesus? Just where do I find the Lord in agony today?

Our contemplation is truly "practical." It is directed toward our collaboration in the divine plan of salvation today. By intently "seeing" and "hearing" Jesus in the great mysteries of his life, we infallibly learn where we are in the continuous unfolding of God's plan. Through this prayer (which Ignatius called "contemplation" and Benedict in the *Rule* for his monks called "lectio divina") we are integrating ourselves into a conversation with God. We become personally involved in sacred history, not out of nostalgia for the past or curiosity about antiquity, but because we have a present role in that history. We are caught up in reality. As long as we live, our lives are unfinished chapters in the amazing history of salvation.

This is not to say that our participation in the saving mysteries is automatic and easy. The dialogue with God may not be to our liking; entering into the living events which involve Jesus is not only exciting, it is risky and challenging. The deepening awareness of Christ's action in our lives may be unsettling, and we have the freedom to terminate the experience. But we also have the freedom to continue the prayer, to remain open to him, to allow him to shape our lives in his image and likeness.

We will inevitably discover areas within us which are not submissive to Christ. Habits must be broken; a style of life must be changed. But there "in the scene" with Jesus, the inanity, shamefulness, and absurdity are more clearly seen. The goal of much apostolic preaching, reform of life and repentance, can be better accepted. And, still mo important, a new direction becomes clear and possible in contemplating Jesus as he lived, died, and rose in glory. "In the picture" with the Jesus of history, we move and feel and respond. We are there to know more intimately, love more deeply, follow more effectively the contemporary Christ, the exalted and glorious Lord of history.

In this contemplative prayer there is a definite movement. First of all, we enter into a certain moment of Christ's life by becoming imaginatively receptive. Then the Lord enters into our hearts and communicates with us. The way he does this may be quite unexpected, perhaps very gentle and quiet. However, there are other factors. We do not go into the mystery with empty hands; we carry with us an awareness of our life and our world. And we do this in order that the Lord may illuminate through this powerful mystery the reality of our social and political existence. "The purpose of this imaginative effort to dispose ourselves aright in prayer is that the power of the Lord's divine initiatives, as received in our prayer experiences, may not be intercepted and turned merely inward, but rather pour itself into the public sphere and make itself felt in the social realities of our time."[7]

A scholarly and critical look at the biblical text is of great importance, and prayer does not dismiss us from doing our homework. But—let us be frank—we dare not remain on the level of historical and linguistic analysis. We are the disciples of a person; it is devotion to the living person of Jesus which is the heart of Christianity. He is active and dynamic. He blesses our scholarship, but he will not be imprisoned by it. His words are not museum specimens. They are spoken to shape our lives, leading us lovingly to the Father and challenging us to serve our brothers and sisters.

This method of contemplative prayer takes us quite quickly beneath ideological matters down to the heart of the gospel, which is discipleship of Jesus Christ and a passionate desire to be close to him wherever he is to be found today. To take the lectionary or the Bible, to read slowly and lovingly the passage which is given to us or which we have chosen, and to enter into that gospel scene in order to contemplate the Lord and dialogue with him may lead us directly into prayers of praise and adoration. We may write down a word or a phrase, but still there seems to be little material for our Sunday sermon. And yet, as we encounter Jesus in this particular mystery of his holy life, we begin to experience in a most profound way what he

is teaching us through this passage here and now. We understand
how it affects us and our people. We cannot escape from the
question of what we are going to do about it. Scholarship, as
necessary as it is, may explain what this passage was saying almost
two thousand years ago. But in contemplation Christ tells us what we
should learn from this event today. We discover its present power. As
Elizabeth Barrett Browning said:

> Earth's crammed with heaven
> And every common bush afire with God.
> But only those who see take off their shoes,
> The rest sit round it and pluck blackberries.

We would never claim that most biblical scholars are content to
pluck blackberries! But it would seem that it is only in prayer that any
of us come to "see" and take off our shoes. It is in prayer that we both
come close to the wordless mystery of divine love and also gain the
courage to talk about what is beyond talk. Prayer somehow makes
possible our strange and wonderful vocation: to speak, with both
humility and passion, about what we have seen and heard, knowing
that it can never be grasped by intellect or language.

HEART SPEAKS TO HEART

He has been called the greatest prose stylist of his century, a time
especially rich in literary artists; he was a seminal theologian with a
broad ecumenical vision; he was, in the words of John Paul II, a
"genius of deep intellectual honesty, fidelity to conscience and
grace, piety and priestly zeal, devotion to Christ's Church and love of
her doctrine, unconditional trust in divine providence and absolute
obedience to the will of God."[8] But for us, John Henry Newman was
most of all a preacher who could arouse in his listeners the desire to
share with him in his vision of heavenly things. As an old lady
remembered years later, "Mr. Newman used often to wear a rather
dirty surplice, but when he read the lessons we thought he was in
heaven."[9]

The motto which he took, *Cor ad Cor Loquitur,* "heart speaks to heart," expresses the goal of Christian communication, what is achieved between Christ and his flock and what we pray to achieve. It is communication at the deepest level: "I know mine, and mine know me." It goes beyond the formal logic of Aristotle which requires words, premises, and conclusions, and is always conscious and verbal; it goes beyond informal logic which is semiconscious and semi-verbal to natural logic which is neither conscious nor verbal. "Heart speaks to heart" when our natural logic concerns persons, when a message is given which is sensed, felt, and expressed in a nonverbal but deeply authentic manner.

Newman was highly intelligent and a master of words—but so were many others. He was an attentive student who, like most other preachers of his time, wrote out his sermons with great care and read them to the congregation. But it was not his thought or his style that was remembered. William Lockhart, who knew him at Littlemore and often heard him preach, said,

It was when Newman read the Scriptures from the lectern in St. Mary's Church at Oxford that one felt more than ever that his words were those of a seer who saw God and the things of God. Many men were impressive readers, but they did not reach the soul. They played on the senses and imagination, they were good actors, they did not forget themselves, and one did not forget them. But Newman had the power of so impressing the soul as to efface himself; you thought only of the majestic soul that saw God. It was God speaking to you as He speaks through creation; but in a deeper way by the articulate voice of man. [10]

John Henry Newman lived a long life, but from the earliest sermons to those he preached as an old man holiness was his favorite theme.

One cannot read any sermons of Newman for the mere pleasure of the thing. That sort of detached attitude is simply out of the question for anyone hearing or reading them. Whether we will or no, we must needs regard them as things addressed directly to ourselves. They put us on our trial, they arraign us, they challenge us in a way that precludes all possibility of slipping away on some side-issue, aesthetic

or other. As someone has said, you could not come away from St.
Mary's without feeling the need of giving up something, of making
some sort of sacrifice, of shaking off the benumbing influence of
habit, and of ceasing to settle down contentedly with one's own
mediocrity.[11]

Cor ad cor loquitur was a principle for his spirituality and his
preaching. For us as for Newman, unless our heart is with Jesus
Christ and we give him our time, our thoughts, and our love, our
preaching will be hollow. We can speak from the heart only about
someone who is near to our hearts. If we only know *about* Jesus and
do not know him, if Jesus and his ideal of holiness do not cause us
delight and wonder in the depths of our being, shouldn't we really
look for other work? For our sermons reveal us. Heart does truly
speak to heart, and we can be exposed as fraudulent and irreligious
or, at least, complacent and superficial. We are unmasked and
betrayed by a tone of voice that is hard and cynical, a gesture that is
flippant, or a posture that is arrogant. Is there an actor or an actress
who could, Sunday after Sunday, hide in the pulpit their true
relationship with the Lord? Newman had nothing to hide. As
Matthew Arnold, the famous critic and poet, said: "Who could resist
the charm of that spiritual apparition, gliding in the dim afternoon
light through the aisles of St. Mary's, rising into the pulpit, and then,
in the most entrancing of voices, breaking the silence with words and
thoughts which are a religious music? . . . Happy the man who in
that susceptible season of youth hears such voices!"[12]
    When I first read W. D. White's tribute to the main qualities of
Newman's sermon, I thought it excessive. Then I realized that it is
merely what all preachers might hope to hear about their work. He
wrote:

> In its fundamental dogmatic basis, Newman's preaching must be
> seen as doctrinal, though not systematic; in its incarnation and
> Christological emphases it is kerygmatic; in its insistence upon
> holiness of life and obedience to the will of God, it is highly moral and
> unsentimental; in its peculiar sense of urgency it is apocalyptic; in its
> awareness of the presence of God and its hope for beatitude it is
> eschatological; in its unrelenting probings of human motives and
> facades it is psychologically penetrating; in its critique of the spirit of

the age it is prophetic; in its urgent longing for holiness and its exaltation of the heroes and martyrs of the faith it is moving and devotional; in its impregnation with biblical and patristic insights and sensibilities, it is genuinely catholic; in its deep sense of the historic church and its worship it is ecclesiastical and liturgical; in its power to *realize* lost causes and forgotten truths, it is superbly apologetic.[13]

The difficulty, of course, with Newman's gifts is that we are tempted to attribute his popularity to his talents, his Oxford education, or the "halo effect" that builds up around a person with his charisma. At the very time that Newman was preaching in England, however, another preacher of far more limited abilities had been assigned as pastor to a little village in a poor section of France. He had done very poorly in his studies and seemed to have no power of assimilation or memory. He was at last accepted for ordination only on the assurance of his old teacher that he was indeed worthy and good; he was also to continue his studies under a tutor. After two years, this unlikely young man was sent to the obscure village of Ars in the dreary flats of the Dombes. The diocesan authorities seemed to feel that he was a suitable pastor for the indifferent and ignorant people of this depressing parish. And there he stayed until his death.

But his likeness to Christ and his insight into human hearts was so great that it seemed as if half of France wanted to talk in person to the *Curé d'Ars.* The name of John Vianney became famous, and fifteen or more hours of his day were regularly consumed by listening and talking to people who came to repent and begin their Christian life anew. And yet, every day he would preach! An English bishop who went to Ars described how the weary Abbé Vianney would stand for a hour at the vestment case in the sacristy carefully writing out each word of the daily sermon. After the hour was over, he would walk to the pulpit and deliver his sermon. The church, small and undistinguished, was packed with visitors and local people who listened in complete silence. However, the bishop indicated, probably no one understood anything! John Vianney read from his recently written text with no attempt at eye contact or vocal projection. By this time he had lost all his teeth, and his voice was almost inaudible. Enunciation was so bad that for almost everyone there the message was unintelligible!

And yet all reports indicate that many hearts were softened, that there were daily miracles of conversion and repentance, and that thousands of people left these sermons with a new zeal for the Christian way. The texts of many of Vianney's sermons have been saved. They are no masterpieces, just conventional examples of piety and the theology of France in the middle of the last century. And they were probably not even understood by many people. Then why? What was the secret of his ministry?

The life of John Vianney "showed Christ," especially the Jesus who set out to seek and save what was lost.

> It is no exaggeration to say of the Curé d'Ars that he gave to his own personal interests absolutely no care or consideration whatsoever; that he put all that he had to give of love and thought and health and strength and time entirely and without reserve at the service of all who needed him—and this for forty long years without respite or relaxation until, at the age of seventy-three, "I can do no more," he said, "it is my poor end.[14]

In the preaching of the brilliant Newman or the far more ordinary Vianney there was a common quality: transparency. Their own faith and goodness were able to be seen. They not only believed and lived as men of the Kingdom—through their absolutely sincere words, their openness and limpid simplicity, the listeners were able to perceive their faith and the attractiveness of a holy life. Even the imperfections in their personalities and, in the case of Vianney, an unpolished and almost inarticulate presentation did not cloud their crystal transparency and the living faith which could be observed. Their power came from their prayer, and in both cases "heart spoke to heart."

A man in Chicago recently said:

> There was an example of good communication at our parish for Good Friday. We took a different approach to the General Intercessions by having various members of the congregation deliver them during the Veneration of the Cross. These people are not accustomed to using a mike and making the petitions out loud in this particular way, or in

this kind of formal setting. So everybody got their petitions 24 hours in advance and they were told to pray over them for 24 hours. Then they were shown how to use the mike and how to deliver them. It was so moving that we had people crying throughout the entire veneration—because these people prayed over their petition. When they came to give a petition, maybe only ten words, it had power.[15]

It is painful to compare the power of these short petitions spoken by a group of lay people with the powerlessness of so many sermons preached by the clergy. Could it be that prayer makes all the difference? Could it be that the long-awaited renewal of preaching will come only when there is a renewal of prayer and holiness among the preachers?

VI. CALLED TO BOLDNESS

Have you ever had the "fif "? No, it is not an illness induced by eating cold pizza or by prolonged study of Hebrew grammar. "Fif" stands for "funny interior feeling" and a goodly number of preachers would claim that it was the beginning of their preaching ministry. Wesley's heart was strangely warmed; Francis of Assisi heard the voice of Christ while at prayer in a little chapel; hundreds of preachers can remember a particular moment on a particular day when they experienced a call which they could not ignore. It was something wonderful and urgent; call it a funny interior feeling, a mystic experience, or the call of Christ, it was real and important for the person involved.

Some denominations are satisfied if future preachers claim to have had that and little else. They have been called by God in a very personal and private way, and that is enough. A pulpit will be theirs. Other Christian denominations may presuppose that there has been an interior call or inclination of some kind, but the call must be tested and confirmed by the proper church authorities. Unless there is a call from a definite Christian community which needs a pastor and a preacher, unless a bishop or a presbyter approves and sanctions it through an official designation or ordination, the interior feeling of the individual, no matter how wonderful and how insistent, is simply not validated.

But whether this call to the preaching ministry is something subjective and unchallenged, or whether it is subject to scrutiny by

seminary authorities and made objective in an ordination ceremony
and the approbation of church officials, there is no doubt that a
preacher must be called by God! "You did not choose me, but I
chose you and appointed you that you should go and bear
fruit. . . ." (John 15:16).

The prophets long before the coming of Christ made it very clear
that they were called, that God had chosen them to be his
collaborators in handing on the divine message to the people of their
generation. It was also made clear that this vocation was neither
sought nor easily accepted. Isaiah, for example, is overwhelmed by
his unworthiness:

> And I said: 'Woe is me! For I am lost; for I am a man of unclean lips,
> and I dwell in the midst of a people of unclean lips; for my eyes have
> seen the King, the Lord of hosts!'
> Then flew one of the seraphim to me, having in his hand a burning
> coal which he had taken with tongs from the altar. And he touched
> my mouth, and said: "Behold, this has touched your lips; your guilt is
> taken away and your sin forgiven." (Isa. 6:5-7)

His lips may be unclean, but he has also seen the King, the Lord of
hosts. His mouth is touched with a burning coal and, through God's
mercy, he is cleansed; he is then eager to be sent as God's messenger.
He is no longer on his own; he is a person chosen by God and sent
forth with his approbation.

Jeremiah drew back from his vocation to preach with the excuse
that he was too young and inexperienced. In fact, he probably was
quite young and without experience, but the Lord God was not
persuaded by his arguments:

> Then I said, "Ah, Lord God! Behold, I do not know how to speak, for
> I am only a youth." But the Lord said to me,
> "Do not say, 'I am only a youth'; for to all to whom I send you you
> shall speak. Be not afraid of them, for I am with you to deliver you,
> says the Lord."
> Then the Lord put forth his hand and touched my mouth; and the
> Lord said to me, "Behold, I have put my words in your mouth." (Jer.
> 1:6-9)

The important point is not the prophet's youth or inexperience or that he seems to attempt the impossible, but that he does not attempt the impossible on his own. He has been called and sent by God, and this suffices.

Ezekiel also is greatly terrified by his vocation: "And he said to me, 'Son of man, stand upon your feet, and I will speak with you.' And when he spoke to me, the Spirit entered into me and set me upon my feet; and I heard him speaking to me" (Ezek. 2:1-2). He is called and sent with great solemnity and there is to be no argument about unworthiness or lack of ability, but, just as with Isaiah and Jeremiah, the preaching task is not his idea! He is not so much a volunteer as a reluctant conscripted soldier, drafted into service by the irresistible demand of God.

One does not decide to become a prophet or a preacher as one decides to be a doctor, a dentist, a lawyer, or an engineer from a list of possible options. It is not a traditional family profession that one accepts because one's father and grandfather had done it. As Amos testified, "I was no prophet, nor have I belonged to a company of prophets; I was a shepherd and a dresser of sycamores. The Lord took me from following the flock . . . " (Amos 7:14).

In some mysterious way, the Lord is taking some of the men and women of today from "following the flock" or whatever might be the contemporary equivalent. A medical doctor gives up a lucrative practice, a West Point graduate gives up a military career, a successful insurance executive resigns to enter a seminary. A talented tenor from the Metropolitan Opera now serves a poor congregation in Peru. Dorothy Day, certainly one of the most powerful voices for the Christian gospel in this century, must sometimes remember when she was a militant Communist editor. But God is no respecter of philosophical systems or of the family business interests; he calls forth those who will communicate his message of forgiveness, justice, and love from some of the most unlikely backgrounds.

Indeed, at the very moment that you read this the Lord may be calling a new Peter and Andrew, a new John and James. The kid working at the gas station and his brother frying hamburgers at

McDonald's may be quietly but urgently asked to leave all that they have and follow him. The salesgirl at Sears and her sister in nursing school find themselves talking to their friends about Jesus. The preachers of tomorrow are being called today. They are those young men and women (and some not so young) who discover that they really care about a person called Jesus, and that they really care about their brothers' and sisters' getting to know him.

They will be touched by and responsible to their age just as they are touched by and responsible to the Lord Jesus. Slowly but surely they will become mature persons, generous and wise. Some will probably become *homines religiosi*, in the sense of Erik Erikson, men and women whose personal and existential conflicts will reflect the conflicts of their age and "push the age along."

They will have a capacity for generativity; they will help their listeners to have life and growth. "I have come that you may have life, and have it more abundantly." Their preaching will help create a climate for personal growth, aiding the listeners to know themselves more and more and to become "new persons" with the help of God. They will firmly hold that within humankind is the potential for growth and change and that, through their preaching, they can prepare people for the life-giving "touch of God." They will affirm that a person is constantly becoming, meant to be a creator of our world, one who is truly "emergent."

Like Jesus, these preachers will have pity on the crowd, ready to pour out their lives to teach them and care for them. They will be true friends, significant others, for the congregation that is entrusted to them. Together they will look at Jesus, "the image of God the Father," to find out who they are and what they should do. Their listeners will know that the shepherds trust them; they will "believe" them into existence and hope just as Jesus did Peter. After Peter's denial, the eyes of Jesus said, "Peter, you're better than that." Caring shepherds call their flocks to something more and something better, not to fear and intimidation.

Growth can come only as a response, so preachers must challenge and question. But this challenging is done as a friend would challenge, bound in a loving relationship. The congregation always senses that it is loved. For a value to become operative, of course, it

THE PERSON IN THE PULPIT

must be incarnated, so those who preach know that they must "enflesh" the Gospel, "embody" the text. They must be able to say as Paul did, "become imitators of me, just as I am an imitator of Christ" (1 Cor. 11:1).

NOT ENOUGH PREACHERS?

Church leaders frequently issue unhappy reports about the small number of preachers. There are so many people who have never been evangelized or are at best semi-evangelized. They may have heard the name of Jesus and know that he existed, but the portrait they have of him is grossly distorted or extremely sketchy. Those who are already Christians need instruction and nourishment for further growth. The fields are white for the harvest, but where are the workers?

How quickly the situation can change, however, when there is a shift in spirituality!

From the first centuries of the Christian experience, spirituality has been grafted onto two different roots. One was Greek, much influenced by Plato, and with a strong resemblance to the oriental mysticism of Buddhism, Hinduism, and Islam. It stressed the individual alone before God, the transcendent, the "other worldly." It had little interest in events of this world, a lack of concern for history. It rather easily slipped into an escape from worldly concerns, even the most terrible and urgent ones. Following Greek dualism, the soul alone was important; the body had best be ignored.

And yet, side by side with it and never completely destroyed, there grew the spirituality of biblical inspiration. It was a contemplation which was historical and committed, deeply concerned with the saving of the whole person. It took the incarnation seriously and reached out to touch the word of life (1 John 1:1). This second spiritual tradition which refused to cut apart the contemplative and active, and which grew so naturally in some of the greatest Christian hearts, is being rediscovered in our own times.

The prayer of Jesus himself becomes a model for our prayer. For Jesus prayed not just in his soul but with his tears over Jerusalem and with his drops of blood in the garden of olives. His prayer was a going out from himself to meet his Father. It was the great act of forgetting himself and in perfect generosity giving himself into the hands of his Father.

Our prayer cannot be a turning in on ourselves, an evasion of responsibility, a kind of self-indulgence. On the contrary, it leads to a crucifixion of selfishness in order to meet Christ and to hear him (Rom. 6:1). It can lead, as John of the Cross noted, through a dark night of the senses, through a loneliness and dryness which purifies us, which makes our selfishness die, and frees us to go out from ourselves to find God.

It is not by chance that the desert is important in the authentic Christian tradition. But it is above all an attitude of the spirit. Jesus (Matt. 4:1), Saint Paul (Gal. 1:17), and so many others right up to our own times have sought out a desert place as an external symbol of an inner attitude of openness and readiness for God. The lonely place of rocks or sand is a powerful symbol of a radical poverty, of a necessary drying up of illusions, of a silence in which we can hear the Word of God and wait in hope for his gift.

But whether the desert place is a hermitage in the woods of Ontario or merely a quiet corner of our house, whether we give ourselves to prayer for a day or twenty minutes, the spirit of the desert means a dying to self in order to live for God and for our brothers and sisters. "Entering the desert" means leaving a cozy world, leaving selfish concerns, leaving a system of comfortable thought, in order to find God and see things as they truly are.

As important as the desert experience is for any Christian, it is of the greatest importance for the preacher. For it is in the desert that false notions and unexamined attitudes are burnt away. It is there that we are freed from conventional wisdom, from the silly slogans of a thousand commercials, from the propaganda of a society which is unjust and deceptive. If we do not get away from the system which has conditioned and softened us, from the oppressive and selfish words which mold our minds and attitudes, will we ever be free to be prophets, to denounce clearly and forcefully what is evil? Prayer and silence which free us from selfishness and from the conditioned reflexes which we have learned in a selfish system will form us as prophets.

And so the preacher goes to the desert, as Jesus did, to return to the people. His or her illusions are gone, and there is a new freedom to preach not only those gospel pages which our society finds consoling and supportive but also those which question and contradict it. Spirituality is understood no longer as a retreat from the truly important issues, but rather involves a commitment to them. The preacher is both contemplative and militant.

Where such preachers are coming forth—persons both of prayer and action—many young people discover that Christianity is far from meaningless in their lives. Where the poor truly have the gospel preached to them, new preachers are called from among the poor. No longer does Christianity lack witnesses.

GOOD NEWS FOR THE POOR

The priest with whom I was staying in Recife suggested that we drop in for a chat with the archbishop. Where I come from one does not "drop in" on an archbishop, but my friend assured me that this one does not stand on ceremony. Indeed, he does not!

We arrived at the bishop's palace, called *Manquinhos*. It was clear that it had once been a pretentious place dating from the days of the Portuguese; but the heavy rains and the hot sunshine of northeastern Brazil had not treated it kindly. People sat on the staircase and along the porch, many obviously ill with swollen legs or distended bellies. We went into the dining room, quite bare except for an old table and chairs, and there we met Dom Helder Camara, Archbishop of Recife and Olinda and one of the most beloved and most hated men in Latin America. In his first sermon, when he arrived from Rio to take charge of this vast diocese in the poor and exploited Northeast, he said:

> The bishop belongs to everyone. Let none be scandalized when they see me in the company of individuals considered unworthy and sinful. Which of us is not a sinner? Who will cast the first stone? Our Lord, when accused of walking with publicans and eating with sinners, replied that it is the sick man who needs a physician.
> Let none be amazed if they see me with individuals considered

insidious and dangerous, leftists or rightists, in power or out, anti-reformist or reformist, anti-revolutionary or revolutionary, men of good faith and bad.

Let none try to confine me to one group or link me to any one party, insist that his friends be my friends and his enemies mine. My door and my heart will be open to everyone, without any exception whatever. Christ died for all men: it is not for me to exclude anyone from this fraternal dialogue.

Have I come to look after the poor? Of course I have, since loving all men, I am bound to follow Christ's example and have a special love for the poor. At the last judgment we shall all be judged according to the treatment we have given Christ, *Christ* in the person of those who are hungry, thirsty, dirty, sick, and the oppressed. [1]

Since the first sermon there have been many others, and while he has endeared himself to millions of poor people in his country and beyond, the rich landowners and politicians are not pleased. Bullet marks can be seen on the walls of the former sacristy where he lives; his life is in constant danger. Only his great popularity with the people has kept him out of prison.

We sat around the old table in the dark colonial dining room, and I looked carefully at this man who is prepared to die for preaching the gospel. He is not handsome and does not look at all strong. He is small, almost like a dwarf, and his gestures are animated in the Brazilian style. He is intense, yet kindly and gentle. His appearance is not impressive. But his words come from deep within him, and he gives his visitor his full attention. He has been called a Communist many times by extreme rightists, but he is equally sharp in his comments about the Soviet Union as he is about the United States. He is not afraid to speak of the causes of poverty in his country, among which are the greed and consumerism of Western Europe and the United States.

His spirituality has not led him away from the poverty-stricken community around him. In a battered Volkswagen driven by his secretary he goes out to visit the people, to preach in the village churches, and to help the poor understand their dignity and their place in the kingdom of God. In his preaching there is no place for a fatalistic acceptance of misery, filth, injustice, and early death.

For Dom Helder and for many other preachers today in Latin

America, it is not enough to read quickly the gospel message about poverty. If the poor are to have the gospel preached to them, evangelical poverty has a place in the life of the preacher. It means that the preacher cannot be aloof but must enter in the struggle for economic justice. He or she must not only speak about the Beatitudes, but must also join the attack against hunger, the lack of housing and health care, unemployment, and the selfishness which causes it. It means identifying with the economically destitute in the way that Charles de Foucauld did in the Sahara, in the way that Dorothy Day does in New York, and Mother Teresa in Calcutta.

It means witnessing to the gospel with a style of life and an involvement in the struggle for justice which is not faddish or romantic, stale or sad. The kingdom of God is full of hope and joy, but it is also clearly against the ways of this world. Those who preach the coming of this Kingdom can expect the wrath of the powerful.

Persecution and martyrdom were not slow in coming in Latin America. If Dom Helder Camara escaped physical harm, many others did not. As long as the church supported the system and preached meek acceptance to the wretched, as long as sermons painted only a suffering Jesus who never rose to victory over sin and over death, as long as religion only meant silent endurance here and "pie in the sky when you die," the clergy were tolerated like loyal old family retainers. Their schools and orphanages could even expect an occasional fat check and the higher clergy a dinner invitation to a seaside villa. But, when preaching brought the people in touch with the living Christ who brings true freedom to the captives and real hope for the oppressed, the facade of religiosity quickly cracked. Modern prophets were standing up in the pulpits of Brazil, El Salvador, Paraguay, and Bolivia. The plans of unjust men were opposed and revealed as immoral. The ministry of the Word was effecting a union with Jesus Christ who wants his "little ones" freed from all bondage, interior and exterior.

THE TESTIMONY OF SUFFERING

Jesus clearly predicted that witnessing would provoke persecution, but for many the old saying that "the blood of martyrs is the seed of the church" applied only to ancient times. Even the suffering of Christians in Nazi Germany or in the Soviet Union seemed to many a special and unusual phenomenon; it could be attributed to an easily identifiable ideology, extreme, odd, and clearly evil. It came as a surprise when Christian prophets began to suffer persecution in capitalistic countries as well, countries that continued to be "friends" of the United States.

In November of 1969, the Brazilian Security Police came to the seminary of São Leopoldo in the state of Rio Grande do Sul. A twenty-five year old seminarian was taken away, arrested on charges of subversion against the military government. Carlos Alberto Libanio Christo was to spend twenty-two months in prison before his trial and then be sentenced to four more years without his guilt having been proven. His parents collected his letters and, although written by a younger man, they have the power of Dietrich Bonhoeffer's *Letters and Papers from Prison* and the *Prison Meditations of Father Delp*. He wrote the following to his brother:

> During these sixteen months of imprisonment I have not yet lost my nerve. At no point have I felt that the past was useless or the future lost. On the contrary, I'm optimistic about both. For me this time in prison is a passage to liberation, a period of waiting for Easter. It counts as a second novitiate, in which I'm reaching a more profound understanding of the mystery embodied in Jesus of Nazareth. Now I know how false are any concepts of God that do not refer to the young man of Galilee. In him I find myself and define myself. But I do realize how ill prepared people are—even Christians—to hear and understand Jesus' summons. Not because his summons is complicated but precisely because it is too simple. It's difficult to come out of the labyrinth into which our traditional conditioning has led us. We aren't yet strong enough to face the temptations Jesus underwent in the desert. We adore temporal power, we look for security, and we fail to grasp how corrupting it is to bow down to the wielders of wealth and power. If we had Jesus' certainty that a legion of angels would come to our aid, we would not hesitate to cast ourselves from the hilltop. But we haven't this certainty, so we prefer to be a legal church rather than an evangelical, endangered church. Clearly the Holy Spirit is working to get the church moving. But I think we tempt him too much, always hoping for *him* to act.[2]

In this passage are expressed some of the important lessons for tomorrow's preachers: the necessity of hope, the "waiting for Easter"; the central place of Jesus as the one in whom we find and define ourselves; the terrible simplicity and challenge of his summons; the need to break with a corrupting status quo and to risk a loss of power and prestige; to pray but also to act. In another letter to Pedro, he said:

> It's almost unbelievable how many churchmen live in a vacuum, isolated in their own utopia. They don't know where Laos is, who the prime minister of Israel is, how much a liter of milk costs, what the average salary is in their part of the country, or what social and health services are available. They don't look for causes, they never ask why, they take poverty and wealth for granted, they find war scarcely objectionable, and they are convinced that good will, patience, and prudence will remedy all ills. How are we to preach the gospel to people who look upon us as aliens, who don't understand our language, to whom we represent another class and a different world?[3]

If his tone sounds accusatory and immoderate to some, the harsh words of a student, it may be good to remember that they were written by a man who saw his fellow seminarians brought back to his cell after three days of torture, saw prisoners pushed to commit suicide, and who himself knew the long days of solitary confinement. Pastors and seminarians, nuns and lay leaders, all Christians who have suffered in the prisons of various countries, have discovered that "good will, patience, and prudence" are not the only virtues to be practiced. There are also the virtues of zeal, initiative, and courage.

THE NEED FOR A NEW KIND OF PREACHER

Unlike Guatemala, Honduras, Argentina, Brazil, and El Salvador, in our country those who preach the gospel have not been beaten up by gangs of thugs, arrested, and sometimes murdered in their churches or on a lonely road. Is it because, unlike Latin America, the veneer of official piety is still in place and the dynamite of the gospel is kept damp and harmless? American churches and their clergy have, by and large, established a rather comfortable and unquestioning relationship with the political and economic system. When the Supreme Court declares abortion to be legal, some of us may become angry, but in a most select and discreet way. There was, of course, the extraordinary preaching of the great Martin Luther King and the example of the clergy who demonstrated for civil rights and for an end to the Viet Nam war, but they were never more than a small minority, barely tolerated by their superiors. There is a complacency and conformity which is much more typical of the American clergy, both Catholic and Protestant (and Orthodox and Jewish).

We are, perhaps, so grateful that we have freedom of worship, that our buildings are not taxed and our seminarians not inducted into the military, and so happy with our generous and gracious friends in the business community that we are not able to look with the eyes of a prophet at the quality of our culture. The fact that certain companies will maximize their profits at the expense of poor and defenseless people here or in their foreign "colonies," that dangerous chemicals will be used and will harm and kill their workers in Mexico or Korea, that slum housing will be tolerated for fat profits and payoffs—all of this seems quite remote from our Sunday liturgy, our own concerns, and the concerns of our people. Even if we do suspect that something is wrong, the problems seem too complex and beyond the influence of our pulpit. We lack hope, not goodwill; zeal, not prudence; courage, not patience. We are afraid to take the initiative.

As Parker Rossman wrote in *The Christian Century*:

> "Of course there is nothing I can do about war," the pastor of a small church declared. "Clergy do not have enough political clout to tackle the major unsolvable problems of the world: disease, pollution, over-population, crime, injustice, war." He may be wrong. It may well be that, where enabling leadership is concerned, American clergy are in a unique, advantageous position, with an opportunity which few other people in the world have. . . . In Russia and in other totalitarian states, both left and right, the most fearless advocates of human rights are usually nurtured in minority religious communities which on the surface have no power at all.[4]

Few preachers can specialize in economics, law, political science, advertising, and sociology. But we must be humble enough to learn some important facts from the experts. We must study and reflect, pray and discuss. We must "see, judge, and act." We may find that capitalism and Christianity are not bound in a loving and inseparable union, that their marriage was not necessarily made in heaven! We may discover that the American way of life is not God's greatest gift to the human race, and that it too is judged by the gospel and found wanting. We may learn that much of our civilization, from the beer commercials on television to the decisions made in the board rooms of our banks and businesses have little to do with Jesus and his Kingdom. Like the prophets who went before us, we too must preach repentance, but—as always—there are many obscenities, and many of them have nothing to do with sex.

Just as we have not seen ourselves as prophets and critics of the American system, neither have we, as American preachers, pictured ourselves as missionaries. It is not that we have lacked men and women who felt called to the missions. But the missions that these zealous Christians went to serve were usually in Asia or Africa. The rest of us stayed at home and tried to conserve a faith that was already there.

In the American tradition, much of Protestantism has been considered almost the established religion of the country, and it is the very nature of an established religion to preserve the establishment. Ministers saw themselves as defenders of solid Pilgrim virtues which were deeply woven into the American *ethos*. Preachers in some denominations were considered the employees of church boards who insisted on a Sunday service that would reinforce their white, Anglo-Saxon, middle-class values. New members who would "fit in" were always welcome, but there was no special urgency to go out and look for them.

Lutheran and Catholic pastors, on the other hand, were kept busy with a multitude of recently arrived ethnic groups. It seemed important to preserve not only the faith which they had brought with them from Europe but also the languages and cultures in which it was expressed. These pastors might be German or Irish, Swedish or

Slovak, Polish or Italian, but all would agree that their first responsibility was to protect the faithful from "falling away" from what they already had. They felt no need to have a "missionary" spirit; young people from their congregations who spoke of such a tendency were shipped off to join some "missionary society" to be trained for China or India.

For both main line Protestants and Catholics, whatever was evangelical seemed in dubious taste, tainted with wild-eyed enthusiasm, and had best be left in storefront churches and tent meetings. The truly solid and respectable clergy were cautious, not innovative. There was no reason to be innovative when pastoral methods were already at hand which had been proven successful and safe. The flock was already in the sheepfold, and the good conservative pastor had only to keep his eye on them.

The church, however, which isolates and confines the missionary spirit is already in trouble. The preacher who ignores evangelization is no longer clearly listening to the voice of Christ. The congregation that does not reach out to those who need the gospel and is content to feed its own piety is not only narcissistic and dull, but unfaithful to the Lord. While we busied ourselves with our loyal lambs and sheep, something important was happening in the United States of America.

Today 41 percent of all Americans over the age of eighteen (sixty-one million adults) are functionally unchurched (i.e. they have not voluntarily worshiped in a church, synagogue, or temple of their choice for six months or more, not counting funerals, weddings, Christmas, Easter, or the High Holydays). In the past twenty-five years there has been a drop of 22 percent of those who consider religion very important in their lives, from 75 percent in 1952 to 53 percent in 1978. Four out of five unchurched Americans today come from Catholic, Protestant, and Jewish families that attend church or synagogue. Seventy-seven percent of them received some religious training.[5]

It has always been recognized that certain spiritual gifts were necessary and certain human characteristics highly desirable in those who would bring the gospel to distant lands. They needed a radical conviction and zeal, a joyful enthusiasm and courage, a flexibility and openness to new experiences, a deep respect for people and a willingness to learn their languages and customs, a resilient faith and a happy and healthy piety. They could not be timid or easily shocked. They had to be people who had an authentic warmth and welcome for strangers and an understanding that the kingdom of God belongs to the poor.

It is now obvious that this becomes the necessary profile of the preacher for today and tomorrow. If we believe the task of evangelizing all people is the essential mission of the church, the virtues of the conservative and authoritative pastor of yesterday are not enough. We must continue as teachers of the faithful and guardians of the Christian tradition, but we are also being sent out to a poor and unbelieving people. They do not know our language or our heritage; they are generally unimpressed with our titles and degrees. They are, however, fairly curious to know what happened to us since that moment we accepted the message we now proclaim. As Grasso has indicated:

> A message spreads to the degree that the messenger is able to make his listeners believe that they, too, can succeed in resolving their problem and in giving new meaning to their lives. The listener surrenders to the values proclaimed when he accepts them as part of his life, but this he will not do unless the witness is able to communicate the claim, the attraction and fascination contained in those values. Such communication is impossible unless the witness has himself had such an intense experience that he cannot do otherwise than communicate it. This means that the attraction which the values proclaimed are destined, by their very nature, to exercise, can be explained and can become real only when embodied in a witness, from whom that attraction can then irradiate.[6]

There is a magnetism about those who are courageous and ready to dare anything for Jesus Christ. In the Acts of the Apostles we read: "Now when they saw the boldness of Peter and John, and perceived that they were uneducated, common men, they wondered; and they recognized that they had been with Jesus" (Acts 4:13).

The people of our own country and time are waiting to be

astonished at our boldness since we also, if not uneducated, are only common men and women. Like themselves, we are wounded and sinful. But they are ready to be startled into attention by the boldness of our proclamation and to be moved by the sincerity of our testimony. Will they recognize that, like Peter and John, we also have been with Jesus?

NOTES

CHAPTER ONE: OUR BIBLICAL JOB DESCRIPTION

1) *Readings in Classical Rhetoric*, ed., Thomas Benson and Michael Prosser (Bloomington: Indiana University Press, 1969), p. 57.
2) *Ibid.*, p. 118.
3) *Ibid.*, p. 136.
4) Robert Mounce, *The Essential Nature of New Testament Preaching* (Grand Rapids: Eerdmans, 1960), p. 84.
5) Grimm and Thayer, *A Greek–English Lexicon of the New Testament* (Grand Rapids: Zondervan, 1956 [1889]), p. 440.
6) John R. W. Stott, *The Preacher's Portrait in the New Testament* (Grand Rapids: Eerdmans, 1961), p. 22.
7) *Ibid.*, p. 25.
8) *Ibid.*, p. 80.
9) *Ibid.*, p. 82.
10) Jerome Murphy-O'Connor, *Paul on Preaching* (New York: Sheed & Ward, 1963), p. 74.
11) *Ibid.*, p. 76.
12) *Ibid.*, p. 76.

CHAPTER TWO: VOICES OF THE PIONEERS

1) Saint Augustine, Great Books of the Western World, Vol. 18, eds., Robert Hutchins and Mortimer Adler (Chicago: W. Benton, 1952), p. 685. Reprinted by permission.
2) *Ibid.*, p. 696.
3) Saint John Chrysostom, *On the Priesthood* (London: Society for Promoting Christian Knowledge, 1964), p. 11. Reprinted by permission.
4) *Ibid.*, p. 12.
5) *Ibid.*
6) *Ibid.*, p. 114.
7) *Ibid.*, p. 116.
8) *Ibid.*, p. 131.
9) *Ibid.*, p. 133.

10) *The Preaching of Chrysostom*, ed., Jaroslav Pelikan (Philadelphia: Fortress, 1967), p. 23.
11) *Ibid.*, p. 24.
12) Saint Gregory the Great, *Pastoral Care*, Ancient Christian Writers Series, Vol. 11 (New York: Paulist, 1950), p. 38. © 1950 by Johannes Quasten and Joseph C. Plumpe, © 1978 by Johannes Quasten and Rose Mary L. Plumpe.
13) *Ibid.*, p. 46
14) *Ibid.*, p. 72.
15) *Ibid.*
16) *Ibid.*, p. 234.
17) *Ibid.*, p. 176.
18) Bernard of Clairvaux, *Five Books on Consideration* (Kalamazoo: Cistercian Publications, 1976), p. 117.
19) *Ibid.*, p. 137.
20) *Readings in Medieval Rhetoric*, ed., J. Miller *et al.* (Bloomington: Indiana University Press, 1973), p. 163; Today's Speech, 17:4 (November, 1969).
21) *Ibid.*, p. 168.
22) *Ibid.*, p. 175.
23) *Ibid.*, p. 235.
24) *The Words of St. Francis*, ed., James Meyer O.F.M., p. 159. © 1952, Franciscan Herald Press, Chicago, Il. 60609. Reprinted by permission.
25) *Ibid.*, p. 269.
26) *Ibid.*, p. 170.
27) *Ibid.*, p. 239.
28) *The Soul Afire*, ed., H. A. Reinhold (New York: Pantheon, 1944), p. 398.

CHAPTER THREE: "WHEN YOU CARE ENOUGH . . . "

1) Milton Mayerhoff, *On Caring* (New York: Harper & Row 1972), p. 2.
2) *Ibid.*, p. 8.
3) *Ibid.*, p. 23.
4) *Ibid.*, p. 59.

CHAPTER FOUR: THAT SPECIAL SPARKLE

1) Alex F. Osborn, *Applied Imagination* (New York: Scribner's, 1963), p. 41.
2) Walter J. Burghardt, "The Word Made Flesh Today," *New Catholic World*, 221 (May–June, 1978), p. 124.
3) *Ibid.*
4) Osborn, p. 218.
5) Karl Rahner, "Priest and Poet," *The Word: Readings in Theology* (New York: P. J. Kenedy, 1964) pp. 9-12.
6) Luis Alonso Schökel, *The Inspired Word* (New York: Herder & Herder, 1965), p. 186.
7) Andre Malraux, *The Voices of Silence* (Garden City, N.Y.: Doubleday, 1953), p. 281.
8) Rollo May, *The Art of Counseling* (Nashville: Abingdon, 1967), p. 78.
9) *Ibid.*
10) Lucien Deiss, *God's Word and God's People* (Collegeville, Minn.: Liturgical 1976), pp. 124-25.

11) A. H. Maslow, *The Farthest Reaches of Human Nature* (New York: Viking 1971), pp. 59-60.
12) Burghardt, p. 125.

CHAPTER FIVE: "CHRIST PREACHES CHRIST"

1) F. X. Durrwell, *The Mystery of Christ and the Apostolate* (London: Sheed & Ward, 1972), pp. 148-49.
2) *Ibid.*, pp. 154-55.
3) *Ibid.*, pp. 156-57.
4) *Ibid.*, pp. 159-60.
5) Sam R. Miglarese, *The Ministry of the Word as Primum Officium* (Rome: Gregorian University, 1978), p. 183.
6) John F. Wickham, "Ignatian Contemplation Today," *The Way*, 34 (Autumn, 1978), p. 36.
7) *Ibid.*, p. 41.
8) From an address given at the celebration of the centenary of the cardinalate of John Henry Newman, held in Rome, May 16, 1979.
9) R. D. Middleton, *Newman and Bloxam: An Oxford Friendship* (London: Oxford University Press, 1947), pp. 12-13.
10) *Correspondence of John Henry Newman with John Keble and Others, 1839-1845* (London: Longmans, Green, Ltd., 1917), pp. 390-91.
11) Louis Bouyer, *Newman: His Life and Spirituality* (London: Burns, Oates, & Washbourne, 1958), p. 182.
12) Quoted by Michael True in "Journal of a Pilgrimage," *Campus Ministry Report* (May, 1979).
13) *The Preaching of John Henry Newman*, ed., W. D. White (Philadelphia: Fortress, 1969), pp. 60-61.
14) R. H. Steuart, "St. John Vianney: the Curé d'Ars," in *Saints Are Not Sad*, Assembled by F. J. Sheed (London: Sheed & Ward, 1953), p. 366.
15) Gerald Broccolo, "People and the Liturgy," *Pastoral Music* (June–July, 1979), p. 13.

CHAPTER SIX: CALLED TO BOLDNESS

1) Helder Camara, *Revolution Through Peace* (New York: Harper & Row, 1972), p. 2.
2) Carlos Alberto Libanio Christo, *Against Principalities and Powers* (Maryknoll, N.Y.: Orbis Books, 1977), p. 173.
3) *Ibid.*, p. 181.
4) Quoted in *World Parish*, 19:173.
5) Quoted from a Gallup Poll study in the *Ad Hoc Committee on Evangelization—Special Newsfeature*.
6) Domenico Grasso, *Proclaiming God's Message* (Indiana: University of Notre Dame Press, 1965), p. 168.

INDEX

Abortion, 115
Alan of the Isles, 44-46
Alcuin, 40
All Souls Church, London, 21-22
Ambrose, 29, 30
Amos, 106
Ansgar, 29
Apollos, 19, 27
Apostles, the, preaching of, 15, 89
Aquinas, Thomas, 11, 44
Aristotle, 13, 99
Arnold, Matthew, 100
Artist, preacher as, 78-86
Augustine, 14, 30-31, 48, 56, 90
Augustine of Canterbury, 29
Auschwitz, 69-70

Bach, Johann Sebastian, 85
Barnabas, 29
Barth, Karl, 70
Basil, 29
Bede, 29
Beethoven, Ludwig van, 74, 77
Benedict, 29, 96
Bernard of Clairvaux, 40-42

Bible, the
  as creative source, 77-78, 79-84
  the New Testament, 14-15, 17-
    18, 19, 20, 27, 61
  the Old Testament, 18, 20, 80-82
  See also Gospels, the
Boniface, 29
Browning, Elizabeth Barrett, 98
Burghardt, Walter J., 75-76, 86

Call of God, the, 104-19
Camara, Helder, 11, 110-12
Canticle of Brother Sun (Francis of
    Assisi), 48
Caring, concept of, and implica-
    tions for the preacher, 51-63
Cato, Marcus, 13, 14
Chaucer, Geoffrey, 77
Christian Century, The, 115
Church and society, relationship
    of, 114-17
Columban, 40
Columbanus, 29
Communications Center, the, San
    Francisco, 71

Guibert de Nogent, 42-44

Herald
  as aspect of ministry, 17
  in kerygmatic theology, 16
  in Pauline writings, 16
  limitations of the, 16
  preacher as, 15-17
  role of the, 15-16
Homiletic services, 74-75

Ignatius of Antioch, 29
Ignatius of Loyola, 95, 96
Imagination
  finding new ideas, 74-78
  importance of, 64-86
  and judgment, 72
  sources of, 67-71
Imaginative preacher, the, 66-72
Institutio Oratoria (Quintilian), 13
Ireneus, 29
Isaiah, 105

Jansenists, the, 56
Jeremiah, 11, 105
Jesus
  ministry, style of, 14-15, 23,
    59-61, 107
  personal encounter with, 89
  and prayer, 108-9
  as savior, 57, 87-88
John Chrysostom, 25, 34-37, 48
John of the Cross, 109
John Paul II, Pope, 98
John the Baptist, 15

Kerygmatic theology, 16
King, Martin Luther, 115
Knowledge, preacher's need for,
    45-46
Kolbe, Maximilian, 70

Leander, Archbishop of Seville, 40
Leo the Great, 29
Lockhart, William, 99
Logos, 13
Luther, Martin, 92, 95

Magnificat of Mary, 81
Malraux, André, 79
Manual for preachers, first organ-
    ized. *See* Guibert de Nogent
Maslow, A. H., 84
May, Rollo, 80
Mayerhoff, Milton, 52-53, 57
Media, use of the, in preaching,
    59, 71
Messiah complex, 56-57
Methodius, 29-30
Miglarese, Sam R., 93
Mozart, Wolfgang Amadeus, 85
Murphy-O'Connor, Jerome, 27

Newman, John Henry, 98-101

Oikonomos. See Steward, preacher
    as
On the Priesthood (John Chrysos-
    tom), 34-36
Osborn, Alex, 72, 77

Palestinian Liberation Organiza-
    tion, 81
Parent, preacher as. *See* Father,
    preacher as
Pasciak, Marc, 82-83
Pastoral Care (Gregory the Great),
    37-40
Pathos, 13
Patrick, 29
Paul
  as father, 22
  as God's coworker, 27

INDEX

in congregation, 56
in Lord, 57
in oneself, 57-58
Trusting preacher, the 56-58

Vianney, John, 101-2
Vietnam War, 115

Vincent de Paul, 26-27
Voices of Silence, The (Malraux), 79

Wesley, John 104
White, W. D., 100-101